2/13.

S-

CUBA and CASTRO

CUBA
and
CASTRO

Teresa Casuso

Translated from the Spanish
by Elmer Grossberg

RANDOM HOUSE • NEW YORK

With my heart full of memories of my own people, I dedicate this book to the people of the United States, whose greatest treasures are their simplicity, their sincerity, their striving for understanding, and their good will.

They always stretched their hands out cordially to me. With affection I stretch out mine to them.

And in my hand is this book.

CUBA and CASTRO

Prologue

New York, November 14, 1960

It is a month to the day since it happened, and now at last the swarm of reporters and photographers has left my house, the continuous ringing of the telephone has stopped, the bedlam of strange sounds and voices and thrusting faces has dissolved. Once more my house is quiet.

It was like a nightmare. Eyes and mouths and scribbling pencils surrounded me while the voices rattled at me: Stand here . . . Smile . . . ("No!") Why did you desert Castro? . . . ("I am not a deserter! He deserted the cause of liberty!") Where were you born? . . . Give some incident from your childhood. Doesn't *anything* stick out? Nothing at all? Think again, there must be something . . . Here, Doctor, it's my turn! Did you have a romance with Castro?

And a dozen people shouting together over the babble: When did I send the letter of renunciation to Castro, what was in it, why did I do it, what is my father's name, what is his work, am I married or single, how old are my parents and where do they live, do I think they are in danger because of what I'm doing, is Fidel Castro a Communist, is Raúl Castro a Communist, is Che Guevara a Communist, is it true they're building a base for launching guided missiles . . .

And all the while the flash bulbs exploded in my face,

3

the television spotlights pierced my eyes . . . flashes and voices and lights and shouts, the phone ringing end-lessly . . . an uninterrupted flow of new arrivals shoving my furniture out of their way, catching some informa-tion and going away, coming back, avaricious, impatient . . . Sounds and emotions clashing strangely, as at a vulgar funeral.

In the midst of it all I could almost see my mother going quietly about her household chores and then sud-denly being brought the unexpected news. How? Who? Who would it be who startled my father as he sat peace-fully in his chair with his newspapers and maps, study-ing the countries of the world and the current inter-national issues now that his only child, his roving Teresa, who had only just completed a trip around the world, was one of Cuba's representatives in the United Nations? Who would it be who told him that the daughter he was so proud of was no longer at the UN, and had broken with the government that had sent her there? I had been unable to prepare them for this, although they had known of my troubled state of mind for some time, since my last visit in June. Always, ever since I was a little girl, they had backed me up, and suffered the consequences. . . . With the reporters asking me about the danger threaten-ing my parents, I put the thought from my mind. This was no time to think of it. My parents had had the same sincere faith in the revolution as the rest of the Cuban people, and it had fallen to me to disturb that faith.

That was the way it went, two, three, four days. The same questions over and over, pinning me to my despair. And there were people who saw a chance to com-mercialize me. It seemed my person had turned into a dollar sign, I was exploitable, because I was suddenly well known, I was "news." I was flooded with offers from literary agents and public relations firms, with invitations

4

to appear on television, give lectures, write articles. My soul flinched at the suggestion that my drama and the drama of Cuba be made translatable into money. I rejected an offer of ten thousand dollars for an article. I refused the protection of the police, for I wished to hide only within myself, to go to a peaceful countryside or far, far away, as far away as I could. But I remained in my house; I understood that I had an obligation to do something on behalf of my people and of the decent people of good faith here in the United States who came to me, not for reasons of money and exploitation, but in order to make some modest contribution to human understanding and kindness. I was tied to this city, to my house, to my telephone, I was at home to everyone, even to those who might wish to harm me. . . . People called me until two, three in the morning, asking questions. Some were men I did not know, inviting me to go dancing. I was assailed by strange offers, effronteries, invitations, and the endless questions. A man wanted to know if it was safe to go to Venezuela on business at this time. Another asked if visas to Cuba were still being granted. Others had legitimate, relevant questions I felt obliged to answer, and I talked and talked, explaining and repeating the same things over and over until my throat was dry and my nerves raw and brittle. . . . Along with the torrent of voices came telegrams and letters and more letters I still have not had time to answer. Only two of them were piously insulting. They hurt even though I was already quite numbed. They hurt me not for myself but for their sincere but deluded authors. It is so hard to fight against fanatical faith!

But the other letters—how kind they were! Some were even written in bad Spanish, as if their authors sought to draw nearer to me through the gentleness of my own language. Natives of this country they were, good

5

honest souls with modest incomes, offering their homes, sending pictures of their children, their houses, God bless them. Are not the people of my own land the same? Why must we have so distorted a view of one another? Why hatred, when there is so much honest love in our two peoples? And there were letters that showed an understanding of our problems and deplored not only the evils that afflict Cuba but the forces in their own country which nourished the roots of those evils. They were spontaneous letters, and assuaged my pain a little: the pain of uprooting myself; the pain I felt for the confusion and suffering of my people divided, my people destroyed by an avalanche of hate.

In Cuba, my parents can no longer send me a letter, or receive one from me. It is possible . . . Already they may have— No, I do not want to think of that, I cannot. I have not the right. When the whole press fell upon me, that morning of the fourteenth of October, I told myself, "Tomorrow I will cry," and went on answering questions while they asked me to smile for the cameras. I must continue to say it to myself, or I cannot go on.

*   *   *

On October 13, 1960, I mailed a letter that changed the course of my life. It was to Fidel Castro, asking him to relieve me of my post of Ambassador Extraordinary and Plenipotentiary of Cuba and Delegate to the United Nations Organization, to which he had himself assigned me. I gave the reasons for my decision and retraced the past that had so closely united us. And this, although it will oblige me to relate many incidents of a more or less personal nature, is what I am going to do in this book. What I saw and experienced in connection with Fidel Castro is, I believe, of general interest, for it deals with

6

the history of Cuba, my little country upon which the eyes of the world are turned, wondering if it is there that the first explosions of a third world war will take place.

I am now living in the United States of America, where there is special interest in what is happening and what might happen in Cuba. The public feels involved; it asks questions, offers solutions. But the majority know little about our problems, whose consequences are already affecting them and are capable of affecting them even more. I believe that an understanding of the conflict between Cuba and the United States is a key to the understanding of the relations of this country and its citizens with the rest of the world. For these reasons, though I have intended this book for the peoples of all the Americas in general, I dedicate it to those of the United States in particular; to the men and women of good will who, like myself, are trying to find answers through understanding and without fear of the truth, without altering truth and converting it into a weapon of malice, misunderstanding, and destruction as those who hold the power in Cuba have done.

Even if this book were published after the present regime had vanished from my country, the lesson Cuba has taught us would continue to have current and future value. The incidents that took place still throb with life and urgency, like their tragic actors both living and dead, for this is the drama and the tragedy of living history. There is in addition, in this drama, a vital protagonist, the Cuban people themselves, who in large part were responsible for creating the circumstances which produced Cuba's most recent leader—Fidel Castro.

I am here going to relate the events I lived through in connection with this central character. I intend to express myself as objectively as I can, but in order to communicate with an Anglo-Saxon people I must ask its indulgence in trying to understand a temperament, and an experience, different from its own. Just as I try to understand you, my American friends, I beg you to do the same. Not to understand is the greatest poverty that can afflict us. And it is our greatest danger.

and the large birds of bright plumage native to the Archipelago, and the abundant shellfish. She put manganese, nickel, iron, copper, chromium, and even petroleum into our portion of earth, and favored the products of its soil—coffee, tobacco, sugar cane, tropical fruits—with high quality and speed of growth. Centuries ago our island was already known as "the Pearl of the Antilles."

Nature gave us many things, not just sugar cane, and it is not her fault that we were robbed and plundered, and coerced into desperately staking our national life on the mercy and fluctuating prices of a single crop.

The indigenes who were the early inhabitants of the earthly paradise they called Cubanacán were peaceful. There was little to terrify them before the Spaniards came. Except for the shark, there were no ferocious or venomous animals on their island. Food and water were plentiful. Today the Indians are gone, the forests are all but gone, the wild deer that ran in those forests have almost disappeared; the few that are left stay in the *sierras*, like the rebels. The shark is still there, but so too are the rest of Nature's gifts: the hummingbird, the mockingbird, the coast-to-coast breeze, the mild year-round temperature, the lovely beaches, the fish in the sea. It could still be the island paradise it was for the Indians and for the early colonists; and that it seemed to be, in recent years, to the many pleasure-bent visitors to our shores, who did not take into account such unwelcome things as poverty, illiteracy, unemployment, corruption, freedom's suppression, and foreign control. The royal palm is still there, that great friend of the peasant, long and slender and with large leaves of brilliant green, standing tall on the plains in clusters that murmur and sway, giving the peasant his house, his roof, protection against lightning, and food for him and his animals. And there is one more thing the island has never lost—its spirit of freedom.

Despite their lack of aggressiveness and their tradition of mild living and peace, our indigenes, the Taínos and Siboneyes, fought the Spaniards who wished to enslave them. Whole villages committed suicide to avoid being conquered; those who were captured died by the thousands, unable to endure slavery. The Indians were exterminated, but their instinct for liberty is still with us, as if it were the one thing that proud people left us to remember it by. For four centuries the inheritors of that spirit fought the colonial tyranny. Then they fought those of their compatriots who wished to duplicate that tyranny. And they are still fighting. There have been times when the fight appeared to have been won, until victory turned into a mirage as a new despot replaced the old. The Cubans have never been free, and this is partly their fault, and partly, as I hope to make plain to the readers of this book, it is not.

Although the modern Cuban has also inherited the Indians' love of mild living and of peace, he has grown accustomed to taking up arms and fighting for his freedom. After so long, it has become an automatic reflex. Despotism invades and robs the peace of the private citizen in a way that Americans have never known, or have forgotten.

Left to himself, the Cuban does not like to fight. On the contrary, Cuba could once have been described, quite simply, as an island peopled with good folk who liked to sing and dance and who had a high appreciation of good humor, jokes, and the expression "nothing's happened," which always ended incipient fights and quarrels. This was the old Cuba so many tourists knew who went there to drink Bacardi and learn the rumba and stretch out on the beautiful beaches. Any difficulty that arose, of whatever nature, led straight to another of our classically optimistic expressions: "There's no problem, no problem at all."

The crime rate was so low you could not fill up a single page of a newspaper with the crimes covering a period of six months. Bloodletting incidents were almost always of the type called "passion crimes" and in any case were so rare that they were talked about for months. It was the same with robbery. The Cuban people are as honest as any in the world. This dominant honesty of the Cuban springs from his sense of dignity, and from a pride of bearing which is one of his fundamental qualities. He feels that to commit a robbery is a confession of defeat or inability. Because he is temperamentally optimistic he scorns the former, and his high work standards rule out the latter. His intelligence coefficient is high, his physical reflexes quick. Foreigners have discovered that our doctors are generally first-rate, as are our workmen. Care, precision, and skill, whether in the construction of houses, the making of clothes and shoes, or mechanical labor, are a point of national pride. We do not tolerate bad work, dawdling, carelessness, slovenliness, or dirt. As for personal cleanliness, it is a national custom to bathe once a day at the very least. I don't think there is a cleaner people on earth, nor one which, in proportion to its population, uses more soap, talcum powder, and perfume.

We are, in fact, perfectionists, and it may be this quality that couples with our extremism to make us rebel, not only against dirt and poor work, but also against injustice, arbitrariness, instability.

And yet, in spite of the Cuban's honesty, scrupulousness, and love of liberty, our history is a succession of despots and dishonest governments; because of those qualities, it is also a history of fierce political struggles to overthrow them and install, once and for all, a truly honest, democratic government. Our flag has a white star of liberty on a red triangle of spilled blood, and five horizontal stripes, three of them cobalt blue for sea and sky, and two of them white, for purity of ideals. Ideals count for much in our country. It was for their ideals that our native-born, the Creoles, fought for reforms, then for independence, and freed their Negro slaves, and fought again for independence—this time economic. It was for ideals that a revolution was fought and won against Batista in a time of prosperity—fought not by the hungriest and neediest so much as by the middle and professional classes, whose goals were the freedoms so cherished by Americans.

This last revolution was another that seemed finally to have achieved those goals, until again they slipped from our grasp—another mirage. Fidel Castro had an unprecedented opportunity to set Cuba on a constructive, democratic road. His personal popularity after the victory was enormous, and undisputed. A whole people looked to him to give it peace, honest government, justice, freedom, self-reliance . . . the very things which his revolutionary movement had promised.

When Castro came down from the Sierra Maestra to enter Havana in triumph, there was much work to do. The per capita income of Cuba's population of 6,400,000 was about six dollars a week. More than a quarter of that population could neither read nor write. Another quarter was only temporarily employed—in spite of the fact that economically it was not a bad year, as sugar had brought a high price. The unemployment is an annual affliction, and arises from the fact that our economy is based on a single industry. A quarter of our labor force finds work during the sugar-cane harvesting and grinding season, which lasts three months, and is out of work for the rest of the year—"the dead season." What the United States went through in the worst years of its economic depression, with a high of 25 per cent unemployment, is a yearly recurrence in Cuba for nine of the twelve months. There was that to do, and more. There were our fine bays and excellent ports which we had never been able to make

14

good use of. First the Spaniards had denied us freedom of commerce; then the Americans had inflicted on us their high tariffs, to our despair—but to their gain. And we had no merchant fleet. As for our fishing fleet, it consisted of a few old patched-up launches which dragged the fish back alive in cages rigged alongside. And the political corruption that had plagued us from the very beginning.

Yes, there was much room for a fresh start in Cuba. And the time had never been so propitious. What we needed was planned construction, controlled reorganization, diversification of crops, economic adjustments with the United States, and gradually to achieve economic independence of everyone, including the United States.

What the Castro regime has given Cuba, instead, are hatred, fear, suspicion, greater economic instability, a police state, and utter economic dependence upon Russia and the Soviet bloc. And critical silence.

Of them all it is the silence that is the most alarming.

The Cuban has always taken refuge from bitter reality in the joke. At the start of the present tyranny, so-called "counter-revolutionary" jokes flooded the island like an enormous festive conspiracy of ironies. Every day they entered into circulation and made the rounds despite the reigning terror. It is what was jocularly referred to as "Radio Bemba"—"*bemba*" meaning "mouth" in the popular vernacular. "Radio Bemba" was a fifth column that no government had ever been able to crush and that reflected the mood and opinions of the people as a whole.

One of the first disturbing acts of the revolution was to set about to change the national idiosyncrasy; it wished to convert the laughing, joking Cubans to "serious," dramatic people. Our humorous newspapers, which had been unique in the world, based on the caricaturing and spoofing of politics and politicians and saying more than any number of long, judicious editorials, lost all their humor and purpose with Fidel Castro's advent to power.

15

It infuriated the topmost leader to be caricatured; he and "his" revolution must be taken *seriously,* by which he meant that all Cuba must stop laughing and joking. He persisted in linking himself—and Cuba—to the tragic severity so visible in the stubborn set of his face. For the first time in Cuba's history our humorous weeklies, with their long Creole tradition, began to be crammed with manifestos and propaganda articles. It was now sacrilegious to express the national humor. The head of the government was out of bounds to any sort of joke—not out of love, but out of fear. Then a great country-wide silence descended, sealing every public outlet. The last time I was in Cuba, in June of 1960, nobody uttered an unguarded word, even in private; nobody commented, nobody laughed or joked for fear of being informed on by friends, neighbors, relatives, and even by members of one's immediate family.

Alarmed, I began to investigate, and saw what was happening, what the government was doing to the people. I saw how already it had begun to seize anyone who expressed a contrary opinion. But it was not only fear that made the people silent. There was also a sense of disorientation, a confused dread of being "counter-revolutionary." For in Castro's Cuba this is the label given to whatever might imply an air of independent judgment, or criticism of some error.

It was then that I began seriously to take stock of our revolution. And I saw that it was passing into the hands of the Communists, who had scornfully stood off from the revolutionary movement until the last moment. Now it was being handed to them on a silver platter by a man with a disordered mind, a man fortunate in war but inept at peace, an absolutist obsessed with power and personal glory.

But communism, with its enforced discipline and regimentation, its collectivism, its devotion to materialism, and its silent obedience to "the leader," can never capture the Cuban people. Repression notwithstanding, the Cuban is too much of an individualist. Political and economic instability have always involved him in his country's—and the world's—politics from childhood, and have made him the living, walking, self-perpetuating image of liberalism and democracy. In the parks, on the buses, on the radio, in the newspapers—wherever he could he talked, discussed, disputed, argued. As a national type he is antipathetic to silent obedience. He is the embodiment of that sense of liberty which is the basis of his joy of living. Through reason and conviction he will accept changes he deems constructive, or he will accept them through love and good faith—but never by imposition. No one has ever been able to mold the Cuban's thoughts through external pressure. If at the moment he is living under a totalitarian regime, he is himself the best, the only antidote to the disorientation that has temporarily managed to superimpose itself on the country, but that cannot penetrate, cannot change its people.

Provided that it has enjoyed democracy at some time, a people that has come to live under a Communist regime will emerge from the confusional disease immune to further contagion. Cuba, therefore, now that it has come face to face with the Communist reality, will be the best "anti body" on the American continent toward the refutation of communism as a form of government.

The calamity that has befallen my country is not an irremediable one. It occurred because democracy in Cuba was not able to function properly at the right time. It was not permitted to.

In this book I wish to explore the part the United States of America played in the events that led us to that democratic failure and, inexorably, to the present unhappy situation.

chapter

2

All our revolutionary struggles over the last thirty years
have had two objectives: political independence and economic transformation. Among the prime requisites of the
latter is the diversification of crops.

Because of the unrivaled quality and yield of our sugar,
the fantastic ease with which it grows in our soil, and because of foreign political imposition, we have been coerced into one-crop cultivation, turning a natural bless-
ing into an economic curse. How did our economic
structure come to be so top-heavy? The answer lies in
the two "isms" of the past five centuries—colonialism and
imperialism.

For four centuries we were a Spanish colony. At first
Spain was interested chiefly in gold and silver, and because we did not have any we were left pretty much
alone, with a certain degree of autonomy which probably
helped in the formation of an independent spirit. But
our soil was fertile, and slaves were brought from Africa
for its cultivation. Left to ourselves for two hundred
years, we developed a balanced rural economy based on
cattle, wood, sugar, tobacco, honey, wax, fruits, and animal breeding. Being strategically located at the entrance
to the Gulf of Mexico, we were on the route of all commerce with the West Indies. Treasure-laden galleons
made Havana their chief port of call on their way to and

from Spain. Cuba's location attracted the interest of other European nations, particularly England.

Realizing what a potential of agricultural wealth there was in Cuba, Spain began to strangle the island with increased bonds and taxation, and to establish monopolies on the island. Her tobacco monopoly soon limited the growth of that industry through a quota system—the first of a succession of quota systems which were to cause us so many headaches. The government stored up tobacco until the desired quota was obtained, and prohibited the growers from selling the rest to anyone else, even burning it if necessary. The merchants prospered exorbitantly. They advanced credit payments to the growers, to be paid off in goods—another evil that was later inherited by the farmers when Cuba became a republic. If the advances paid out during the year exceeded the portion of the quota that was finally bought from them, the growers fell into debt. The debts accumulated from year to year, and the cultivators' poverty increased. This led to the first rebellion, the Uprising of the *Vegueros* (tobacco growers) in 1717, against taxation and for freedom of production and commerce. The revolt brought promises, which were not kept, and our first strike followed. Fierce skirmishes ensued between the cultivators and the "scabs" and strike-breakers sent into the fields. Then came bloody repression.

The pattern was set. In succeeding centuries it would change in scope and intensity, but not in essence. At first the demand was for freedom of commerce, then for autonomy, and finally for independence. The theme of economic strangulation or freedom remained the same. It ran through "The Big War" of 1868, which lasted ten years and failed, and "The Little War" of 1879, which lasted one year and failed, to the War of Independence in 1895, which lasted three years and triumphed.

Spain lost all because, being absolutist, she wanted all.

19

The same thing happened with England and her American colonies. England's colonials, with their more democratic and autonomous tradition as Englishmen, and with their Protestant self-reliance, were able to be the first to achieve independence. In so doing, they avoided contracting many of the public vices and corruptions which inevitably harm colonial countries. And they acquired at the same time vigor and strength, while, however, still lacking the maturity to employ those qualities judiciously. Strength tends to expand itself, and this they began very quickly to do. With countries as with men, youth always lacks the responsible thoughtfulness needed to restrain its excess energy. As a result, the United States, which should have been like a big brother to us when we were taking our first toddling steps as a new republic, became instead a bully with a "Big Stick" and replaced Spain as our chief nemesis. Later you will see why I say this.

The English colonials, born on American soil, were called Yankees. The Spanish colonials who were born in Cuba (or anywhere in the New World), were called Creoles. The Creoles of Cuba took root in the land and became cultivators and property owners, while the Spanish-born, called "Peninsulars" after the physical shape of Spain, engaged in commerce. The Peninsulars worked in close collaboration with the authorities, and their loyalty remained with Spain and the Empire. The Creoles, on the other hand, became the foundation of the new Cuban nationality. Toward the end of the eighteenth century there was a great liberal advance made on the island. French enlightenment darted through Europe, and progressive governors, reflecting the liberal influence in the metropolis, arrived from Spain and launched projects of public improvement. More schools were built (Havana had had a university since 1728), newspapers were founded, printing and publishing establishments were

20

set up, books were more widely distributed. A population census was taken; cultural and economic societies were formed. And out of this a brilliant group of progressive and cultured people emerged, a generation of Creoles educated in Europe or in the European manner and especially influenced by the liberal, intellectual climate created by the democratic revolutions in the world sparked by the French Encyclopedists.

The Creoles carried the ferment of the struggle for liberty, and from their ranks came the impetus for insurrection and movements for independence. Rich, educated, this new nationality produced many outstanding personalities in the first third of the nineteenth century. The Creoles studied their country's problems thoroughly, and the world's; they initiated progressive movements, fought for reforms and for freedom of commerce; they headed the resistance to the monopolists, and, eventually, contributed entire fortunes to the wars of liberty. Many wealthy Creole landowners voluntarily impoverished themselves for the cause of freedom—freedom for the less fortunate cultivators and the Negro slaves as well as themselves—in short, for their ideals.

From the early part of the ninetenth century the lines of division were beginning to be drawn. The Creoles ranged along the political scale depending on how far they believed liberalism should go. Some wanted only minor reforms of a commercial nature. Some wanted autonomy, and to keep their slaves. Others wanted separation from Spain and annexation to another, larger, slaveholding country, the United States—and this is where the United States, as far back as the Jefferson Administration, first comes into the Cuban picture. Still others were for total independence, and for the abolition of slavery as well. Some of this last group of landowners and intellectuals were jailed or executed for aiding a revolt of the Negro slaves in 1812, a revolt which was bloodily suppressed. Desperately opposed to liberation of any kind were Spain and the Peninsulars. Spain was in the process of losing the vast southern part of the American continent to the insurgent armies of Simón Bolívar, and was determined to hold "the Pearl of the Antilles," and at any price.

Spanish oppression became increasingly ruthless, and in 1868 our first war for independence broke out. It was called "The Big War" or "The Ten Years' War." It started with an uprising on a sugar plantation led by its owner, a lawyer of distinguished family and education, Carlos Manuel de Céspedes. Like the rich landowners of Camagüey and Oriente provinces who immediately joined forces with him, he freed his slaves. The rebels took an important city, Bayamo, near the Sierra Maestra, and so began a heroic epic that was to produce many battles and deeds of glory, and the most romantic figure of our wars of freedom, Ignacio Agramonte. This young man gave everything for liberty, including his life. His valor and nobleness were so legendary that when the Spaniards killed him in battle they were afraid to give him a grave, and burned his body.

The Ten Years' War came to an end in 1878 when the exhausted, impoverished, and decimated Cuban forces finally had to accept a truce. In 1879 fighting broke out again in what was called "The Little War," which lasted a year. The rebel leader was Calixto García, a man known in the United States as the recipient of the "message to García."

After that, Cuba lived through a restless period of conspiracies and abortive revolts, of discouragement and division brought on by the successive defeats. The U.S. government did not look favorably upon the designs of the Cuban emigrants in the United States to send expeditions and arms for the continuation of the struggle. The reason for the government's attitude was that the struggle was for total independence, and not for annexation to the United States, whereas U.S. governments since the time of Jefferson had been maneuvering, sometimes secretly, sometimes openly, for annexation. The South, in particular, saw an opportunity to avail itself of another slave force.

It is thanks to José Martí, who made his appearance on the world scene in that discouraged hour of Cuba's history, that we were able to fight and win the three-year struggle that brought us our independence. He called it "the necessary war." Despite the fact that the U.S. government had its fleet patrol the waters to prevent shipments from reaching Cuba, even going so far as to seize our ships and enormous quantities of munitions and equipment; despite the bitter divisions among the revolutionaries produced by the previous defeats, this man of singular faith and personal power, the greatest man our country has produced, managed to unite all Cuba. He reconciled the oustanding leaders of the past wars, traveled all over the American continent collecting volunteers and aid for the cause of Cuba's liberation, and organized our War of Independence.

José Martí was a great poet, lawyer, and man of letters. He was an impressive orator, and an exceptional political analyst. Moreover, he set an example of humanism, kindness, and self-sacrifice that inspired others to give the best of themselves. His erudition embraced all branches of human knowledge. Because his mind bypassed a country's borders he was able to write on all subjects—and always with clear foresight with regard to the future of Cuba and the American continent. Even in Spain he was admired and respected by all he met.

He lived in the United States for a time, and knew and loved the country for its many virtues; and he admired its great men. And of all this he wrote. As an on-the-spot observer he reviewed that interesting period in American history, and in his concern for the American people and for his own people he foresaw, again, the future of our relations. Martí was the mentor of the Cuban nation, its highest expression, its best guide, its most unforgettable force. We call him "The Apostle" because his life was an example of apostolic gentleness and of the capacity to love, understand, and build. All Hispanic culture recognizes in him its most illustrious American. The importance of this tribute is best understood when one realizes how many great men have been produced by the Creole branch of the Spanish culture.

When Fidel Castro triumphed, those who did not know him well believed him to be another José Martí. To me this seemed an irreverence that made me blush for shame. With the written thoughts of Martí we have fought tyrannies when other weapons were not available. Today an army of those thoughts stands opposed to Fidel Castro hand in hand with his own people. Martí wrote:

"Liberty is like genius, a force which sprouts from the unknown; but genius like liberty is lost without the guidance of good judgment, without the lessons of experience, without the peaceful exercise of the criterion."

The War of Independence began in 1895. Three months later Martí was killed fighting on our soil.

The War lasted three years and produced incredible feats surpassing even those of the Ten Years' War. The greatest single exploit was the sweep across the length of the island that was called the Invasion. Starting in Oriente Province, at the eastern end, and moving westward, the insurgents fought their way forward inch by inch in unrelieved combat until they had carried the war to the end of the westernmost province of Pinar del Río. It took a year to do, and counts among the most extraordinary military feats of all time. At their head was General Antonio Maceo, "the Titan," a handsome Negro of great intelligence and a veteran of the Ten Years' War. Spain

24

sent its best generals and two hundred thousand soldiers to halt the drive. General Martinez Campos, military strategist and Governor of Cuba, tried to contain it by placing his troops in the narrowest parts of the island, but could not stop the Titan. He was defeated in battles in which he had an overwhelming superiority in men and arms. Turning back from Pinar del Río to attack Havana, Antonio Maceo was killed eighteen miles outside the city. It was a hard blow for the Cuban forces, but just as the death of Martí had failed to destroy the work he himself had begun, so the death of General Maceo became only another inspiration for the rebels. It was too late for anyone to impede the Cuban drive for freedom.

Governor Martinez Campos decided to leave the island, and said: "I take with me the Spanish flag." U.S. envoy Stewart L. Woodford, in Madrid, reported to Washington: "They know that Cuba is lost." In a last-ditch attempt, Spain sent General Valeriano Weyler as Governor. Weyler, a man hardened and calloused by the wars in Africa, ordered what was called the "Reconcentration." Cuba's entire rural population was evacuated to cities and towns in order to prevent the insurgents from receiving food and aid and to force the population into a mood of surrender. Abandonment of the countryside made the devastation of the island almost complete. The Spanish army carted off our whole rural population in a biblical exodus of men, women, children, and old people, who camped in the streets, only to die of hunger and epidemics. The inhabitants of the cities, already impoverished, were barely able to help that starving mass of humanity that lay dying in the streets.

A million persons died as a result of the Reconcentration. Newspaper accounts of that episode shocked the world. The U.S. Consul, Fitzhugh Lee, also protested, denouncing the horrors of Weyler's government. But, though all Cuba starved, the people did not surrender.

25

The Queen asked the Pope to arbitrate the dispute. The Pope refused. As a last recourse the Crown offered autonomy. It was too late for that. The rebels rejected autonomy, and at the same time opposed the United States' intention to intervene in a war which was at the point of being won. They had an army of over 53,000 men. The sentiment of the Cuban leaders and of the Government-in-Arms was that if the United States wished to help the cause of Cuban liberty it could send arms, but it must not intervene militarily.

Nevertheless, the United States intervened, refusing to recognize the Cuban Government-in-Arms. It found a pretext to enter the war and at war's end three months later took over control of the island, disbanded the rebel army, and dictated the terms of the peace.

Why did the United States do this? To what purpose?

This is the other side of the coin, the converse of this history. It begins far back and ends with the Spanish-American War and the American occupation of Cuba. It is a deplorable thing, and it is the seat of our troubled relations in this century, and of Cuban instability. Neither you nor we Cubans of today are responsible for that history. We were not there. But it is necessary to approach the past honestly and to search out the truth. It is also necessary to incorporate that past with general world history, and to see the events as the product of their time and of factors converging to make things happen as they did. It is the chapter of this book that is the hardest for me to write and for you to read. The American public has a general lack of comprehension and of information regarding our past relations. Those relations must be clarified if we are to try to find remedies for our present ills.

After my appearance on the "Meet the Press" program, I received many letters, most of which were stimulating and informed. But there were also several which took cordial, regretful issue with me on certain remarks I made concerning U.S. policy toward my country. I was reminded that the United States had liberated us from Spain and given us our independence, that it had not kept Cuba for itself when it could have done so, and that it has always tried to help us. . . .

To those who believe these statements, I especially dedicate the next chapter.

chapter

3

With Europe and its colonialism gone, a new form of colonial activity—imperialism—arose from our own community of nations. And it came from the North— from the United States of America.*

Imperialism is definable as the expansion of capital which, having achieved tremendous breadth and force, bursts out of the interior economy of its country of origin and spills over the national borders to invest itself in other countries. That is to say, instead of taking physical possession of those countries, it takes possession of their natural wealth. It does not stop to consider that the rights of some end where those of the rest begin, or that as Benito Juárez of Mexico said, "Peace is respect for another's rights." It is not concerned with moral right and wrong.

A country that dominates the economy of other countries is naturally a determining factor in their life and politics, and just as naturally tries to exert ever-greater influence over their destinies—destinies that will, after all, affect those investments. For its own protection the investor nation needs political control of the countries in which it has large economic interests. As a result of

* Professor Herminio Portell Vilá's voluminous *Historia de Cuba en sus relaciones con los Estados Unidos* has been a valuable source of information for the material in this chapter.

having permitted its large enterprises to invest in our countries, the U.S. Government is obligated to intrude in our internal politics and in the official policies of our governments. But we, though poorer and weaker, have a right to the self-determination of our countries. We freed ourselves, after much suffering and at a high price in human lives, from a colonialism far less liberal and more crushing than that of the English. We have earned the right of our own sovereignty. But the health and potential strength of this sovereignty was gradually undermined, step by step, through more than a century of time, in proportion as Latin America was invaded and finally overrun by those "pioneering" forces of North American capital which now no longer risked life and limb, which no longer represented a high standard of human courage, or signified anything other than the fact that it was frankly and shamelessly motivated, with the right quite simply of might, by acquisitiveness.

When the infant republics to the south opened their eyes and started trying to walk on their own legs, they found that their own principal economic resources did not belong to them. This one fact is responsible for the malaise characteristic of this century and especially of recent years in the relations between the United States and Latin America, where U.S. private investments amount to approximately 9.5 billion dollars.

About a quarter of all U.S. exports goes to Latin America, from which it gets a third of its imports. But what the United States acquires from us is almost always *raw material*, which is processed and made into finished products, many of which are then imported by us at high prices and with payment of high tariffs. Most important, we lose the opportunity to give our people the jobs and wealth that the industrialization of our raw materials would bring to our countries.

There lies the "cause of complaint," as well as the

main reason for the poverty of Latin America. In the economic sense it is still a colony, providing raw materials, lacking industrialization and technological development, its agricultural potential controlled and limited, its soil worked for the benefit, not of the majority, but of a few proprietors with immense tracts of land. The attempt to introduce agrarian reform collides with interests established by the United States in the past and brings intervention of one kind or another.

In 1920 two thirds of Cuban land was the property of U.S. companies, along with most of the sugar mills; along with the gas, electric, telephone, and transportation companies; along with whatever railroads did not belong to the English; plus almost all the industries, such as there were. All that is important to a country, all its wealth and productivity, was in the hands of U.S. enterprises, from whom we bought almost all our imported goods. A revolt against this state of affairs would have risked putting us into their hands even more completely, thanks to a document called the Platt Amendment, which gave the United States the right to intervene in Cuba to preserve order and guarantee the security of its properties and investments. Where did this Platt Amendment come from? From a long history of maneuvers by the United States to take possession of our island. Why did we tolerate the drawing up of such a document, and put our name to it? Because we had no choice.

From the time President Jefferson first toyed with the idea, the annexation of Cuba to the United States was a pet project of successive American governments right up to the twentieth century. President Madison sent "explorers" to Cuba on "missions of good will," while a correspondent and State Department agent named Shaler was in Cuba making contact with Creole annexationists. In 1823 Monroe maintained the Union's interest in the island even while keeping Europe at respectful distance with the Monroe Doctrine, whose two main points were summed up in the popular slogan "America for the Americans." (We of the southern part add with irony: "—of the North.") And in subsequent years it became abundantly clear that the United States did not want the independence of Cuba, but the annexation, which for reasons of mutual gain attracted both U.S. and Cuban slaveholders. For John Quincy Adams, Cuba was an "apple that had to fall by gravity into the hands of the United States."

In 1844 commercial relations between the two countries were so close that 40 per cent of Cuba's total imports came from the United States, and 20 per cent of her exports went to her growing neighbor. Cuba was the United States' most important market after England and France.

When Polk advanced the expansionist program by annexing Texas, New Mexico, California, and the northern part of Arizona to the Union, the way seemed clear for the incorporation of Cuba. The Theory of Manifest Destiny was in full play. The apple seemed ready to fall. Polk ordered the expeditions leaving for Cuba from the United States to be crushed, and sent a special envoy to Spain with a purchase offer. The language of expansionism of that period wore a pretty veil: each annexation was referred to as "extending the area of Liberty."

Polk's successor, Zachary Taylor, halted the purchase negotiations temporarily, but in 1853 President Pierce renewed them with an offer to the Queen of Spain of 130 million dollars—representing an increase of 30 million over Polk's offer. As the rift between North and South widened, however, the North began to denounce all attempts to annex Cuba, while the South continued to try desperately to neutralize the Union's newly incorporated abolitionist states by acquiring one with its own economic

31

structure. Pierce was obliged to shelve his purchase plan, and a bill for the purchase of Cuba presented to Congress during Buchanan's term of office was likewise defeated by the northern states.

In Cuba, too, the annexationist movement came to a virtual halt at about this time. It had had the support of a good many Creoles until they came to understand that this was not the answer to Cuba's problems. José Antonio Saco, one of our most brilliant men of the nineteenth century, whose essays on slavery, the Cuban economy, and the country's needs were published around the middle of the century, wrote a study of annexation that gave this idea the death blow as far as Cubans were concerned. A short paragraph from that study will demonstrate his foresight:

"The triumph of annexation . . . would bring to this island a new culture, elements of a new race and a new foreign power, an overlord with its own interests, different from and opposed in many important ways to those of the Cuban people."

The case of Puerto Rico is an excellent illustration of Saco's foresight. Like Cuba, it fought bitterly for independence, only to become part of the booty of the Spanish-American War. In the case of Puerto Rico, however, possession was formal and permanent. For many years it has been a living example of the result of the dramatic collision of two different races, religions, languages, cultures, and traditions. That result was so disintegrating—even its language was corrupted into a lamentable linguistic hybrid—that in recent years a more practical policy on the part of the United States, which had become aware of the negative results of its previous one, has granted that island a certain autonomy as an "Associated Free State." The Puerto Ricans are now having a revival of Hispanic culture, and new national forces are recapturing much of what was lost. This has been accompanied by a sharp improvement among the population, which had found itself without a true identity, disoriented, unassimilated, converted into a kind of social pariah debased and disdained by its new "mother country." The United States had finally understood that the island, which was never even given the status of a State of the Union, had sunk into a decadence disadvantageous to all concerned. Pretty much the same thing, incidentally, has resulted from a similar clash of language and race that has taken place in the Philippines. However, it is pertinent to add that the United States is aware of its errors of the past and is doing what it can to rectify them. For Cubans, to deny this is sheer demagoguery—or a nationalistic blind spot, the product of an inferiority complex which utilizes past injustices and outrages to wage present crusades of hate.

The terrible period following the Civil War found the United States absorbed with its internal problems, while Cuba was battling through its "Big" and "Little" wars with Spain. Toward the end of the 1880's the United States was again wearing its iron-heeled seven-league boots. Cuba, on the other hand, was ruined. Its wars had devastated the countryside and the economy, and had impoverished most of the landowners. This was the propitious moment for the healthy young American dollar to step in and to buy up extensive properties and utilities, as well as sugar plantations.

The United States was now entering a period of great economic and financial growth, and was developing a plutocracy which, if it was not formally at the controls of the democratic vehicle, was nevertheless the engineer whom the government had always to consult—and, in important matters, to obey. It was this driving economic force—the power behind the throne—that went exploring voraciously in all directions and built railroads, established telegraphs, commenced the exploitation of mines, the cutting down of forests, the sowing of huge areas with wheat and beetroot, and undertook an aggressive campaign of foreign investments. In their effort to dominate Latin America, these powerful interests coined a word which they were to use for their exclusive convenience: "Pan-Americanism." For the rest of the globe the United States was still satisfied with the ring of the words "Manifest Destiny," as it established itself on some of the Samoan Islands in the Pacific and, in 1893, on Hawaii.

In the last quarter of the century American investments in Cuba already amounted to 50 million dollars —a considerable sum for those times. Families named Atkins, Farrell, Havemeyer, to name a few, had the Sugar Trust, engaging in both planting and refining—that is, the sugar was planted in Cuba and refined in the United States. The Pennsylvania Steel Company, the Bethlehem Iron Works, and the Carnegie Steel Company acquired iron, chromium, and manganese mines. By 1894 Standard Oil held the monopoly in Cuba of petroleum and its various derivatives (kerosene, etc.). American capital was invested in electricity. In addition, the United States deepened its economic entrenchment on the island by placing high tariffs on Cuban refined or manufactured products, such as sugar. It imported almost the whole of our annual output of raw sugar, but put high tariffs on our refined product, and in this way Cuba's own refineries were put out of business while the colonial nature of her industries —as a producer of raw materials only—was accentuated. It was the same with the tobacco industry. By means of high customs duties protection was given to raw and withheld from manufactured tobacco. This resulted, among other things, in a large-scale emigration of skilled tobacco workers to the United States in search of work, most of them settling in Tampa, Florida.

Noting that the economic well-being of Cuba was coming to depend more and more on the United States, José

34

Martí declared: "Economic union means political union. The people that buys, commands. The people that sells, serves. It is necessary to stabilize trade if liberty is to be assured."

Toward the end of the 1880's the American press began actively warming the public to the idea of the possession of Cuba. From the more or less secret government plans and machinations the affair moved into the public eye. Newspapers discussed how to accept Cuba, or whether to accept her at all. On March 6, 1889, the *Manufacturer*, of Philadelphia, said: "The only hope we might have to qualify Cuba for the dignity of Statehood would be to Americanize her completely, covering her with people of our own race." The article went on to demean us as a people, even going so far as to describe us as effeminate. José Martí responded by pointing out the historic virility of a country that had so continuously and courageously fought for its liberty. One of the things he brought to the attention of the *Manufacturer* in his demand for respect was the respect we had always shown for the people of the United States. He reminded the editors that that generation being reviled by the newspaper was the same one that, braving the anger of Spain and the majority of slaveholders, wore mourning bands for a week following the death of Abraham Lincoln.

The New York *Evening Post* opposed the purchase plan—on the grounds that the United States ought not to burden itself with "inferior races."

Shortly before our War of Independence began in 1895, José Martí and his followers suffered their worst setback in the United States when three ships laden with arms and military supplies were seized and impounded. That the war was able to get under way at all was due to the indomitable perseverance of Martí and his patriots, who, with the important monetary help of the Cuban tobacco workers in Tampa, finally succeeded in getting some expeditions through.

When the Cuban insurgents finally rejected Spain's offer of autonomy, U.S. Consul Fitzhugh Lee, thinking we would not be able to endure the horrors of devastation and Reconcentration we were being subjected to by General Weyler, saw in the unpopularity of autonomy a return of the annexationist opportunity. Immediately there was an offensive on the part of the purchase lobbyists in Washington, with one Samuel Janny, of 6 Wall Street, at their head. Here for the first time we have the undisguised appearance in our history of Wall Street, which has had so much to do with the destinies of Cuba, the Americas, and the world. By the end of the year the U.S. Government was again persecuting and seizing our expeditions. Presumably its intention was to thwart a conclusive victory by the Cuban forces that had felt strong enough to reject Spain's offer.

On December 6, 1897, in his Message to Congress in which he declared that "God Himself" had favored him "with a Divine Revelation to take over the Philippines," President McKinley had this to say in referring to the Cuban situation: "We have the desire to see the Cubans prosperous and contented, protected in their right to reap the benefit of the inexhaustible treasures of their country." Those "inexhaustible treasures" were to cost us very dear, now that ambitious eyes were fixed protectively upon them. In this same message McKinley threatened either to recognize the belligerents or to intervene in order to terminate the war. American intentions were thus made clear three months before the battleship *Maine* blew up in Havana Bay.

From January 11, 1898, there were ominous movements of the American fleet. On the twenty-fifth the *Maine* entered Havana Bay despite Consul Lee's advice not to send it and his warning that incidents must be avoided. On the twenty-seventh the Navy Department ordered Commodore George Dewey, chief of the naval squadron in Asiatic waters, to be prepared to act at a moment's notice. The "Divine Revelation" of McKinley was being converted into a plan of action to take control of the Philippines, with Cuba as the pretext.

Worried by the triumphant sweep of the Invasion forces across the island, Weyler's withdrawal, and the prospect of Spanish defeat and Cuban independence, the commercial Peninsulars of Cuba began frantically conspiring with the Americans to bring about annexation. Theodore Roosevelt was already preparing for a possible attack on Cuba. Consul Lee reported anti-American riots on the island. It was at about this time that U.S. envoy Stewart L. Woodford, in Madrid, informed Washington that the Spaniards knew that Cuba was lost.

On the night of February 15, 1898, a great explosion shook the city of Havana. The U.S. batttleship *Maine* had exploded in the Bay. All its occupants perished. And this was the spark that inflamed the people of the United States to a point where they were now ready to go to war in Cuba, as the slogan "Remember the Maine" raced over the country.

There had been 260 men and one officer on board the battleship. All the rest, including Captain Charles D. Sigsbee were ashore that night. At first the captain and Consul Lee accused no one, and said they believed it was an accident. Then came the accusations that the explosion had been intentional. Spain indignantly rejected the accusations and appointed a technical commission to investigate the cause of the explosion. The U.S. government did likewise, and the two commissions gave opposite judgments, the Spanish commission claiming that the explosion had occurred in the ship's interior, and the American, that it had been caused by a submarine bomb placed under the ship.

The facts were never ascertained. But the truth was that Spain had no desire to provoke a war with the United States; the last thing she wanted at the moment was a conflict with so large an enemy, whose intentions regarding Cuba were well known. The Cuban independence-fighters, for their part, were opposed to America's entry into their war and would not have committed so provocative an act. Besides, the history of our wars for independence had been characterized by a tradition of chivalry toward the Spaniards to a degree that would have made such a deed unthinkable.

Hardly had the explosion occurred than the American press rocked the country with a campaign for intervention. The New York *Journal* and the New York *World* increased their circulations enormously. Hearst's *Journal* more than doubled its circulation in one month to over a million.

On March 1, 1898, Lee sent a dispatch to the State Department, where the occupation of Cuba was under consideration. In the dispatch was the following comment:

"American capital and enterprise would soon Americanize the island and the immigration would be so great that when the question of annexation would have to be considered the Cuban population would not be much of a factor in the problem."*

A very different note was struck by Senator Redfield Proctor after a visit to Cuba: "To me the strongest appeal is not the barbarity practiced by Weyler nor the loss of the Maine . . . but the spectacle of a million and a half people, the entire native population of Cuba, struggling for freedom and deliverance from the worst misgovernment of which I have ever had knowledge."† Also in con-

---

* *State Department Archives,* Havana, Vol. 132 (Lee-Hay, March 1, 1898).
† Speech in U.S. Senate, March 17, 1898.

trast to the prevailing annexationist or imperialist attitudes ("The war in Cuba must stop"), were those of various New York newspapers like the *Herald*, the *Evening Post* and the *Times*, who, in their editorials, advised the annexationists in and out of the Federal Government that the Cubans were fighting to be free and not to be incorporated into another country.

Nevertheless, the combined offensive of government, press, and public opinion culminated in McKinley's War Message to Congress on April 11, 1898, in which he called for military intervention in Cuba and declared that it was not prudent "to recognize at the present time the independence of the so-called Cuban Republic." In reference to that message, Henry Steele Commager has said:

"In this message to Congress, President McKinley recounted the events which in his opinion justified intervention in Cuba. Filled with suggestion and innuendo, the account is thoroughly misleading, but it struck a responsive note in Congress and in the public mind. Inasmuch as Spain, in the note received by McKinley April 10, promised to order an immediate cessation of hostilities in Cuba, the principal basis for intervention had disappeared."*

Congress began work on the Joint Resolution, taking care not to give the Cuban Government-in-Arms official status or to mention it by name. The most it permitted itself to say in the first of the original three articles was: "The people of Cuba is, and by right should be, free and independent."

The second article warned Spain to abandon the island. The third authorized the President to utilize all sea and land forces and to raise a militia to be sent to Cuba.

Four Democratic senators of the Senate Foreign Re-

* *Documents of American History*, ed. by H. S. Commager (New York: F. S. Crofts & Co., 1935), Vol. II, p. 182.

lations Committee asked that the following paragraph be inserted in the Joint Resolution: "And that the Government of the United States hereby recognizes the Republic of Cuba as the true and lawful Government of that island." The proposal was not accepted, and the Resolution went before both Houses meeting together in order to avoid the risk of its being rejected by a third of the Senate.

Because the proposal of the four senators had been rejected, Senator Henry M. Teller, of Colorado, proposed an amendment committing the United States to respect Cuban right of self-determination. After a turbulent debate it was accepted as Article IV of the Joint Resolution. It was worded as follows:

"That the United States hereby disclaims any disposition or intention to exercise control over said Island except for the pacification thereof, and asserts its determination, when that is accomplished, to leave the government and control of the Island to its people."

The press protested and made a great to-do over the Teller Amendment. Grover Cleveland, McKinley's predecessor in the White House, was indignant at its passage; he described the Cubans as "the most inhuman and barbarous cutthroats in the world."

There is a terrible document which everyone interested in knowing the truth about our treatment in the past and about the U.S. Government's attitude toward the Cubans in those years ought to be made acquainted with. It is reproduced in *Liberty—the Story of Cuba,* by Horatio Rubens. Rubens was an American lawyer and railroad magnate who was considered Cuba's best friend. He acted as our lawyer throughout that period, and was known among us by his national nickname, "the Friend of Cuba."

The document I refer to consists of the instructions from the office of the Assistant Secretary of War, and signed by J. C. Breckinridge, to General Nelson A. Miles, Army Chief of Staff, concerning Cuba, Puerto Rico, and the Philippines.

". . . Cuba, with greater territory has a greater population than Puerto Rico. Its population consists of whites, negroes, Asiatics and their mixtures. The inhabitants are generally indolent and apathetic. It is obvious that the immediate annexation to our own federation of such elements would be folly, and before so doing, we must clean the country, even though it be by applying the same means which were applied by the Divine Providence to Sodom and Gomorrah.

"We must destroy everything in range of our guns, we must concentrate blockade so that hunger, and disease, its constant companion, may sap the civilians and cut down their army. The allied [Cuban] army should be employed constantly in reconnaissance and rearguard actions, so that they may suffer rigorously between two fires and to them shall fall all dangerous and desperate enterprises. . . . We will aid with our arms the independent government which will be constituted, although informally, while it is in the minority. Fear, on one hand, and their own interest on the other, will cause this minority to strengthen itself, making the autonomists and the Spaniards [Peninsulars] remaining in the country to appear as the minority.

"When this moment arrives, we should create difficulties for the independent Government, and these, and the lack of means to comply with our demands and the obligations created by us, the war expenses and the organization of the new country, will face them. These difficulties should coincide with the troubles and violence among the elements referred to and to the Opposition we should lend our aid.

"Summing up, our policy should always be to support

41

the weaker against the stronger, until we have obtained the extermination of them both, in order to annex the Pearl of the Antilles."[*]

Let us now observe how these instructions coincide with the actual developments that took place when the United States entered the war:

There was a total blockade of the island, intensifying the hunger of the already impoverished population.

The Cuban ports were bombarded, without any intention of disembarkation, including Matanzas, Baracoa, and Santa Cruz del Sur. All were undefended. Three hundred shells fell on the open city of Cárdenas.

American disembarkation was effected only in those places where the Cuban revolutionists were strong and able to be of assistance.

Besides the regular troops who disembarked with Cuban assistance, there were the irregular troops, such as the Rangers and the Rough Riders. It appears that the suggestion made by the brother of Jesse James, i.e., to send cowboys to "put an end to the war," was being followed. These irregular troops did not obey the official plan of attack but did as they wished, and this created internal conflict among the Americans.

The Cubans, who knew the terrain and the enemy they had fought and defeated during a period of several years, offered co-operation and counsel in the military operations. But General W. R. Shafter later abandoned the plan formulated by the Cuban General Calixto García— and accepted by the United States—for the attack on Santiago de Cuba. Shafter also maintained a great rivalry with Rear Admiral W. T. Sampson, the Squadron Commander. The dissension that existed between the two commanders led to strong personal attacks and insults,

[*] *Liberty—the Story of Cuba,* Horatio Rubens (New York: Brewer, Warren & Putnam; 1932), pp. 344–5.

Shafter calling his rival "damned Yankee." Shafter's tactics cost a great many American lives that need not have been lost. But then, no American lives at all need have been lost, if instead of intervening in our war the United States had limited itself to sending war materials to the Cubans for their final drive. It is not Cuban ingratitude to say this. We know why the United States wished to participate directly. It was in order to retain rights, and to try to exercise control over our independence and our national life. Subsequent events and the history of nearly sixty years of Republican Cuba bear this out.

Spain sued for peace on August 12, 1898, after its naval defeats off the Philippines and Santiago de Cuba, and the surrender of the Spanish garrison in Santiago. Despite the fact that the Cuban army, with over 53,000 men had contributed more than any other land force in the war with Spain, it was at once prohibited from entering Santiago de Cuba, and was not allowed to participate in the surrender conference. Cuba was then militarily occupied by U.S. troops. Our Army of Liberation was dissolved.

On December 10 the Treaty of Paris was signed, giving the United States possession of Puerto Rico, Guam, and the Philippine Islands. Mr. McKinley's "Divine Revelation" had been fulfilled.

As for the Cubans, they simply went on fighting for independence—this time with the Government of the United States of America. A Cuban commission headed by Calixto García went to the United States, and the Americans were astonished to find those Creole leaders to be capable, well-educated, refined people. García, representing the unrecognized Cuban Government, impressed them with his perfect English, his elegant figure, his impeccable manners—and particularly with the firmness of his defense of our rights.

The United States named a Military Governor for

Cuba, John R. Brooks, an honorable and courteous man. In contrast to the eagerness of the U.S. government to portray our Creoles as fierce "natives" badly in need of civilizing, Brooks described them as the chivalrous, self-contained gentlemen they were, who had not the least desire to engage in reprisals against the defeated Spaniards. The Americans, at the end of their Revolutionary War, had divided up thousands of English-owned farms in Virginia, New York, Pennsylvania, and Maine, precipitating the emigration of a hundred thousand English sympathizers. But in Cuba, once the army of Peninsulars was withdrawn, the Spaniards and even the Cubans who had fought with them in the detested "Volunteer Corps" were allowed to remain and live as any others, running their businesses as before. This attitude of pardoning and forgetting was a national characteristic for many years, until the lessons of bloody dictatorships imposed on us the disagreeable obligation to exercise sanctions.

Brooks chose a Cabinet composed of Cubans, and established an amicable and effective relationship not only with them but with the whole population. His attitude had a lot to do with the fact that there was no upsurge of resentment in that difficult hour. His reports were favorable to our people, emphasizing our virtues and the spirit with which we set about rebuilding our devastated country. He was loved by the Cuban people, but not by the American imperialists, who found him unsuitable. Their intrigues continued, and he was replaced by Leonard Wood, the first of Cuba's tyrants after the departure of the Spanish governors.

Wood was arbitrary, cynical, unscrupulous, and adept at intrigue. He employed all these qualities in his corruption of the island and in creating problems among the Cubans. Our historians are agreed that he planted a swarm of evil habits in the bloodstream of the new nation. Like all dictators, he created the public works that give them the glitter they need to distract the public's attention, as well as the opportunity to rob great sums of money under cover of huge budgets, inflated bills, and non-existent costs. He did all he could to obstruct the advent of the Cuban Republic. His letters reveal that he held conversations with Spaniards continuing to reside in Cuba about whether Cuba ought to be given its independence. He did this in spite of the existence of the Teller Amendment in the Joint Resolution.

During Wood's governorship the Cubans were convoked for the drawing up of their first constitution. But the U.S. government immediately put the constituents into a terrible dilemma: the United States would not leave Cuba unless the Platt Amendment was accepted.

The Platt Amendment solved the American problem of how to leave Cuba without actually leaving—that is, without giving up the right to return on the pretext of "safeguarding" the interests of both countries. The Treaty of Reciprocity, together with the Permanent Treaty, in which the Platt Amendment was to be included, converted Cuba into an economic dependency of the United States. In addition to the threat to remain in Cuba, the United States had another one which it used with great effectiveness. I quote part of a dispatch sent by American Minister Herbert G. Squiers to Secretary John Hay:

". . . In this connection I desire to say that a few hints given in the proper quarters would cause an active agitation for annexation, an agitation that those connected with the present government dread exceedingly and which would very promptly force the government to an acceptance of our proposals."*

After almost three months of futile resistance, the

State Department Archives.

Cuban members of the Constituent Assembly saw that they must either accept the Platt Amendment or forfeit a Republic of Cuba, and they gave in.

According to the Platt Amendment, Cuba could not make treaties or alliances with any foreign nation, or grant to any country except the United States—which obtained them for a negligible annual payment—military bases, quarters for troops, or control of any part of the island. "The Government of Cuba consents that the Government of the United States may exercise the right to intervene for the preservation of Cuban independence and the maintenance of a Government able to protect life, property and individual freedom, or by failure of Cuba to fulfill the obligations of the Treaty of Paris for the United States, which will now be assumed and guaranteed by the Cuban Government."

Spanish reparations were not for mutilated Cuba but for the United States, which had arrived at the last minute to wage a brief war of three months, while we were burdened with the commitments of a treaty in which we did not take part.

Cuba was obligated "to execute and carry out sanitation plans already begun, for the health of the people and the commerce of Cuba, as well as for the commerce of the Southern parts of the United States and the population residing in them." We had to be very careful not to infect this powerful neighbor—who desired to trade with us, not only with every economic advantage (one of its first measures was to reduce the tariffs on importations from the island, without giving any reciprocal advantages to Cuba) but with guarantees for its health.

Cuba was also prevented from contracting public debt "if the ordinary tax collections of the island are inadequate."

Finally, we were forced to grant naval bases. There was

even an attempt to make Havana an American naval base.*

The acceptance of the Platt Amendment, of which I have given only the principal points, reassured the expansionists that they would not have long to wait, and the military occupation was lifted in the expectation that our failure would make us drop into their hands, like the apple of which John Quincy Adams had spoken. The elections were finally allowed to be held, and the first President took office on May 20, 1902.

That the dominant idea, despite everything, had been, and continued to be, annexation is clearly shown in Leonard Wood's correspondence with Theodore Roosevelt. Here is part of a letter dated Havana, October 28, 1901:

". . . There is, of course, little or no real independence left to Cuba under the Platt Amendment. . . . She cannot make certain treaties without our consent or borrow money beyond certain limit, and must maintain certain sanitary conditions, etc., from all of which it is quite apparent that she is absolutely in our hands and I believe that no European government for a moment considers that she is otherwise than a practical dependency of the United States, and as such is certainly entitled to our consideration.

"With the control which we have over Cuba, a control which will soon undoubtedly become possession . . . we shall soon practically control the sugar trade of the world or at least a very large portion of it. I believe Cuba to be a most desirable acquisition for the U.S. She is easily worth any two of the Southern States, probably any three, with the exclusion of Texas . . . and the island will, under the impetus of new capital and energy, not only be developed but gradually Americanized, and we shall have in time

* *State Department Archives,* Cuba, Notes, Vol. 1, Q.

one of the richest and most desirable possessions in the world."*

The U.S. troops were gone, but four years later they were to return when there was political agitation in Cuba as a result of the second presidential election.

And this phantom of intervention was for several decades to menace the Cubans who desired to rebel against governments that, with the exception of the first, were all dishonest. These governments loaded the country with American loans—in defiance of the Platt Amendment's stipulation against contracting public debts beyond the capacity of the island's *ordinary* tax collection. They authorized profitable concessions for the American monopolies. They facilitated American economic penetration. Thanks to such co-operation, those enterprises were permitted to do what they could not do in their own country. They could violate customs duties, pay their workers with credit coupons, pay miniscule wages, and continue taking over large tracts of land.

And the Cuban people could do nothing about it, for fear of that terrible phantom of intervention.

But José Martí had written: "The enemies of a people's freedom are not so much the foreigners who oppress them as the timidity and vanity of its own sons." It was as if he had known that our own chief executives were going to give us almost half a century of corruption and betrayal and even, finally, bloody tyranny. But the timidity of a generation of decent Cubans discouraged and afflicted with the trauma of "the Americans are coming" was to end with the emergence of a new generation, "the generation of the Thirties." It was to end when the sons of those soft-spoken Creole gentlemen, and of the Spaniards who had stayed on in Cuba, began their struggle to change things in our country; and when a Cuban President,

* *State Department Archives*, Roosevelt Papers—Wood Files.

48

Gerardo Machado, began to employ a weapon intolerable to the Cuban people—assassination and terror.

And by then our irrepressible island had grown tired of fearing the bogey of American intervention and rose up clamoring once again for freedom, for the independence it had fought for, and won, but had never obtained.

chapter

4

In the first quarter of this century it was impossible for one to become President of Cuba without what came to be known as "the support of the Americans." Without it the most popular politicians could not hope to be nominated as a candidate for that office, regardless of which party he belonged to. The Americans would single out the politician most likely to co-operate with them, make him a partner in one of their enterprises, and then give him their all-important backing. The army, whose officers came from the wealthy families of Cuban high society, did the rest. It always supported the successful candidate, meaning the one the Americans backed, and "kept order" at the polls and elsewhere, seeing to it that the vote-counting and all the electoral swindles went as planned.

In the four-year presidential term, not only the President but his closest collaborators grew rich, as did the professional politicians in charge of the enormous bureaucracy of public employees. This official bureaucracy (there is no civil service in Cuba) was a sort of employment agency and a weapon in the hands of these professional politicians. They prospered in their government positions, handing out jobs in exchange for support and votes. Because of Cuba's insufficiency in sources of employment, there was a great demand for these jobs. The mass of office holders had to fight to survive the inevitable transference of power whenever the party in control was replaced, and so became a defenseless herd maneuvered at will by the politicians. They were made to attend meetings and rallies, and when elections came up, they surrendered their voting licenses to their chiefs to use as they saw fit.

The people, of course, were well aware that the elections were a farce, but felt helpless to act, as rebellion would have provoked an American intervention, as well as persecution by the authorities.

In 1925 the Electric Bond & Share interests gave their support to Gerardo Machado, after first taking the precaution of making him an associate. Among other things, this enabled them to hold the electricity monopoly in Cuba, and to charge fifteen cents a kilowatt hour in Havana and up to twenty-two cents in the Republic's interior.

Machado plundered Cuba with zest. He misappropriated public funds, and weighed the country down with an enormous foreign debt. Despite the Platt Amendment, the American banks loaned him as much as he asked for, and his machinations for paying the huge interest on those loans always victimized the people. Twice he restricted the production of sugar—an expediency which has been one of the favorite resources of our dictators and has always been disastrous to Cuba. The second time, it was in accordance with a plan put forward by an American banker named Chadbourne, and gave the American beetroot industry an opportunity to develop and gave other countries as well the impetus to expand their sugar production and to compete with us. Furthermore, Machado was not content with his term of four years. In 1927, when he had been in office two years, he instituted a constitutional change lengthening the presidential mandate to six years.

As part of the protection that Machado accorded to the foreign interests—the American and Canadian banks

51

which at the height of the Great Depression came into possession of a great many mortgaged sugar mills— cane cutters like those of the Half Moon Central sugar mill in Oriente Province worked from sunrise to sundown at a salary of five cents a day. There was no such thing as maximum working hours or the right to strike. Machado was also partial to the Spanish tradesmen and to native businessmen, guaranteeing them the right to exploit their employees and to persecute whoever tried to organize a union or a strike. Intellectuals were hounded for protesting against his manhandling of the Constitution to extend his powers. The university professors were personally appointed by him, and dissident students were expelled.

Machado was re-elected in 1929.

Before his re-election, he made a "triumphal" visit to the United States, which gave him its wholehearted approval and support, and on his return had all the schools in Havana send their students to greet him with flowers as he stepped ashore. In my school too this order was given. But the students of the University of Havana had visited the schools and indicated that such an order ought not to be obeyed, and I did not go. It was my first act of civic rebellion and the first of the headaches I gave my father, who received a letter from the directress demanding an explanation for my absence. He did not give it, nor did he reproach me. At Machado's disembarkation there was, of course, a huge parade of public employees.

The university students began playing an increasingly active role in their country's politics. Since 1923 Julio Antonio Mella had been stirring up his fellow students by proclaiming in manifestoes and public meetings the truth of Cuban politics and of its colonial position, and demanding autonomy for the university. As an official institution without autonomy, the university—at that time still the only one in Cuba—was ruled by the party in power, which dragged it into the national political corruption, toying with its budget, policing its halls, imposing its politics upon it, or closing it down altogether. Then in 1927, with Machado in office, the students formed the first Student Directorate for the orientation and guidance of Cuba's youth. Machado's response was to install policemen in the university's halls. Three years later, in 1930, the students formed another Directorate. On the morning of September 30 of that year the students, joined by intellectuals of all professions, gathered before the university to protest against Machado's university tactics. The students ran through the streets shouting protests until the police wagons arrived and began carting them off. None of the students was armed, for at that time we did not dream of such things, but this did not prevent a policeman from manhandling one of the members of the Directorate, Rafael Trejo, then firing a fatal bullet into him. Another student, who rushed to help his fallen comrade, received a blow on the head from a mounted policeman which left him bleeding and unconscious on the sidewalk. The name of this second student was Pablo de la Torriente-Brau, and he was to become my husband.

I had known Pablo since I was seven years old, when we had gone to Oriente Province, where my father was going to build a railroad. Pablo was then seventeen, an extraordinary boy both physically and mentally. He used to gather us children together and tell us the heroic stories of history and literature—the Iliad, the Odyssey, the Crusades, the deeds of the noble knight Bayardo and of "the Cuban Bayardo," Ignacio Agramonte, our romantic hero of the Ten Years' War. He read us the children's stories of José Martí, and recounted the lives of the world's great men, making them live again for us.

Or he would talk about boxing champions, or baseball. And it was I who was his most attentive listener.

There in the jungles of Oriente, Father was my teacher, for there was no school. As in the other regions we were to live in during my wandering childhood, I accompanied him on his explorations of nature and learned the countryside, the care and cure of animals, the names of plants and flowers and trees. I was his assistant in healing the sick and wounded. Haitians and Jamaicans would come to us with terrible machete wounds, inflicted as they fought to open breaches in the forests. Father dressed the wounds while I handed him the materials. That was when we lived in the house of cedar, and the mountains burned to make way for sugar cane, and the beat of the bongos came to us from the immigrants' shacks. Father gave me my first horse, and taught me to ride. And he taught me not to admit fear. I saddled and bathed and combed my horse myself, and rode and jumped him over the tree stumps that covered the clearing around the little settlement of bungalows. Soon it was one of his greatest sources of pride that there was no horse, no matter how spirited, that I was not able to ride. He invited the peasants to bring me their liveliest horses, assuring them that I would not be thrown. And he taught me something then, something I have had to repeat to myself many times in my life in order to keep up my courage. As I mounted the restive animal —and they brought me every fiery devil—he would say this to me: "Whatever happens, remember—never throw yourself off the horse."

My education in Oriente may have lacked the formal atmosphere of a school, and it may not have been complete, but it was in many ways an enviable one. And then, there were the stories of Pablo . . .

Then we left Oriente, and I did not see Pablo for several years. We went to the province of Pinar del

Río. There, on our tobacco estate, which was so pretty and full of trees, Father taught me not to be afraid to walk alone in the forest; or to fear the dark, or the phantoms that, according to the neighbors, peopled the house we lived in—an old, oversized mansion, surrounded by rose bushes and flowers of every tropical kind. Wherever we lived, Mother and I always left a garden behind. It was there that the peasants came home from the fields at night singing their intimate, haunting Moorish laments, the *décimas*.

I am relating these things because I was asked to tell of my life, too, in this book, and because I am sure that much of this early formation is directly connected with my later actions.

I am reminded once again, as I write this, of my father's injunction. When I was deciding to withdraw from the government of Fidel Castro I had to consider a dreadful possibility: was I throwing myself off the horse? But I knew it was just the reverse, and that the one who had jumped off was Fidel Castro. Like the Cuban peasants, I am still astride that tired but resistant old horse that is my people's struggle for liberty.

When we returned to Havana I was eleven, and like any girl of the tropics, I looked more like a woman than like a child. Pablo had enrolled at the university as a part-time student, and was at the same time working as a reporter. The work of Pygmalion went on, and at the end of a year that romantic youth had fallen in love with his Galatea. To you it may appear incredible, but when I was twelve Pablo asked my father for my hand.

It caused consternation in my family. My parents, who loved and admired Pablo, tried to make him see reason, asking him to wait until I was graduated from the university. But Pablo assured them that if they did not allow him to marry me when I was fifteen he would abduct me. I was fascinated. Naturally I knew nothing of love, but already that winter I had put on long stockings and stealthily worn my mother's high heels. My good father did not know what to do, for Pablo was like a son to him and to my mother. She it was whose diplomacy finally brought about an agreement. I would be allowed to marry at the age of fifteen. "Not another day" would he wait, said Pablo, pointing out that his grandmother had been very happy and she had been married at twelve; and that my own mother had wed my father at the age of fifteen.

Thus, when we again left for Oriente Province, where my father was going to lay out a suburb next to a lovely village beside the sea, I was declared "engaged." I was told to forget about a career—up to then my parents' dearest wish because of the recurrent sugar crises and my father's financial worries—and to learn to cook and sew instead. But I hadn't the least aptitude for the domestic skills, skills which baffled and terrified me, as my mother well knew. In Oriente I was not allowed to go out or even to speak to a boy. "She is engaged," my parents would say to those who wished to befriend me.

After six months of embroidering and trying to learn cooking recipes, without the presence of Pablo's strong personality, I had enough of being "engaged" and began to feel an aversion for the replies I had to write every day to his beautiful long letters of love. My letters became so empty and brief that Pablo—who was truly the most intelligent person I have ever known—understood there was nothing to be done. He wrote my parents a very sweet, sad letter saying I was a little bird that needed freedom, and freed me from the engagement. Then, ten months later, we returned to Havana, in order that I might acquire a formal education and prepare myself for entering the university.

My father's fears had been realized. Another sugar crisis had tumbled the country's economy and taken his fortune. So that I might continue my studies, he took an engineering post with the government. My dearest wish was to study medicine, as so many of the paternal side of my family had done with eminent success. (There is a Casuso Pavilion at the University of Havana.) But it took too long to become a physician and my father was anxious for the future. He wanted to see me secure in some profession as soon as possible. Mother, who wherever we might be living taught others to read, formed children's clubs, and wrote and improvised verse for all occasions, wished me to dedicate myself to teaching. She herself had always wanted to be a teacher. From her family's tradition of poets I had inherited a love for literature, which Pablo had deepened, and facility for writing, and eventually we compromised: in additon to pedagogy, I would study philosophy and letters.

I was enrolled in a private school, where a preliminary examination showed me to be excellent in history, geography, literature, anatomy and spelling, and terrible in everything else, particularly mathematics. My poor father, being a good mathematician, felt like a failure. Before starting school I spent some time visiting my mother's father in the tiny village near Havana in which I had been born. My grandfather told me about my ancestors from the highlands of Spain—Santander Province—and about a remote ancestor on my mother's side who was not a Spaniard but a Frenchman. It seems that this Frenchman was not an honorable gentleman—in the opinion of my grandfather, who frowned on the enthusiasm I showed for the renegade—but an intrepid pirate named Julian Subirán Laferté. He was supposed to have deposited a fabulous treasure in the Bank of England in the eighteenth century. It is said they are now looking for his descendants named Morín. Well, if any of the English gentlemen of the bank should happen to be reading this, here is one: Teresa Casuso Morín.

In the private school in Havana I went through three elementary grades simultaneously, running from one classroom to another, in order to level off my uneven education. I finished elementary school in six months and went on to normal school for teachers, after passing the entrance examination with the highest mark of all the examinees in Havana.

Pablo, who had resumed his visits to our house when we had returned from Oriente, had also resumed his offensive of books, poems, and flowers. No girl could have long resisted such a charming courtship, and for me he was a magician who rendered everything beautiful and noble. So that I might feel proud of him, he became a rugby player (and was named an all-Cuba guard) and also published a book of stories which he dedicated to me thus: "To Teté Casuso, *muchacha.*" ("*Muchacha*" means "girl," and "Teté" is how Teresas are affectionately called in Cuba.) Many people in Cuba still call me "Teté Casuso, *muchacha,*" remembering those days when Pablo and I were together. In addition, Pablo pursued his studies at the university, and at the same time continued as one of Cuba's best journalists.

Both as a student and as a reporter Pablo was in the thick of the political agitation to clean up the government and free Cuba from its colonial status. Soon after the closing of the university and the student demonstrations which hit full stride after the murder of Rafael Trejo in 1930, Pablo was in prison for his political activities. He and the others of the Student Directorate were imprisoned without trial for fourteen weeks. (He never forgot our "important" dates, and even managed to send me a bouquet of flowers from La Cabaña prison.) After his release, both the agitation and the police persecution continued relentlessly, and when he had been at liberty for some six months he was imprisoned again, along with his close friend Raúl Roa, and the two were eventually sent to the Isle of Pines Penitentiary. He was not permitted visitors, but was allowed mail, and this time not a single day passed without his receiving a letter from me. His book *Model Prison,* written soon after his release, bore the inscription; "To Teté Casuso, who wrote me a letter every day of the five hundred that I was a prisoner." In 1933, when Machado's regime was tottering and he thought it expedient to free his political prisoners, with the understanding that they go into voluntary exile, Pablo and the other students were released and shipped to the United States.

Machado fell when the Americans withdrew their support from him when they thought there was no other solution. Cuba was going through a grave economic crisis, reflecting in large part the Great Depression in the United States. Sugar still hovered near its 1932 low of one-half cent per pound. The Cubans were not buying; for one thing, they did not have the means, and for another, the people had discovered that the boycotting of goods—especially American—was an effective way of debilitating the dictatorship. The public employees had not been paid for months. Unemployment and discontent reigned in all branches of business. Sabotage was a serious problem in the factories and large industries. Although there was no armed revolt, a few uprisings had taken place and had been bloodily put down at their inception. A whole people was in unarmed rebellion. Secret conspiracies abounded, impatient to provoke new uprisings. The Platt Amendment was being defied (and would eventually be repealed).

Another reason for the discontinuance of American support of Machado was that with the inauguration of Franklin D. Roosevelt the United States was introducing a much-needed "Good Neighbor Policy" to replace that of the "Big Stick." Accordingly, Undersecretary of State Sumner Welles was sent to Cuba as Special Ambassador to try to mediate the convulsed country toward a "peaceful solution" that would avoid the outburst of a revolution. The American economic interests in Cuba were stronger than ever before, and a revolution must be avoided at any cost.

While the American Special Ambassador held conferences with the government leaders and the opposition, the secret labor unions called a general strike. The unions were secret because they had been declared illegal and many of their organizers had been murdered. The Communist Party, whose leaders were now the only experienced organizers available in the camp of the workers, directed the strike. The mood of desperation was so general that the whole country joined in. On August 7 there was a false rumor that Machado had resigned from office. The people spilled toward the presidential palace and a massacre followed that made things even worse for the government. By now the whole island was in a suicidal frame of mind. At this point Machado gave in to the workers' demands, whereupon the Communist directors ordered the general strike to end and the workers to return to their jobs. But the Communists had badly miscalculated the mood of the people. For the Communists it was "not worth the trouble to change from one American puppet to another"; but for the workers, Machado was intolerable in any shape or form, and they ignored the back-to-work order. The rest of the population joined them in proclaiming that they would not resume their labors until Machado was out.

Sumner Welles, closely connected with Machado's highest officials, had little trouble persuading them to deliver a *coup d'état* in the form of a polite request to Machado to leave the country, with the guaranty that he and his family would be treated well and their properties protected. Accordingly, on August 12, 1933—the anniversary of Spain's surrender in the Spanish-American

60

War—Machado, his family, and his most important collaborators left Cuba by plane for the United States. The Commander of Machado's army, General Alberto Herrera, became the President for a few hours; then Carlos Manuel de Céspedes, the son of the Cuban patriot of the same name who in 1868 initiated the Ten Years' War, succeeded him as arranged. Welles appeared to have obtained his "peaceful solution." Then something went wrong.

As always happens when there is total ignorance of a people's deepest problems, those responsible for this neat "arrangement," including the Special Ambassador, suddenly found themselves confronted by a broken dike. In the name of its foraging enterprises, the government of the United States had for years supported a bloodthirsty dictator and pillager of the public treasury, and only succeeded in filling the dam till it burst. And the violence it sought to avoid overflowed, whereupon those interests were endangered to a greater degree than if the United States had supported a democratic regime and recognized the right of a people to protect its interests and guarantee fair treatment and just reward for its labor.

With Machado gone, hysterical mobs seized the minor assassins of the fallen regime and dragged them through the streets. They hunted them throughout the land. In Havana the corpse of Machado's Chief of Police, who, when cornered, had killed himself, was hanged on a post in front of the university. The mob sacked the houses of the rich *Machadistas*. Valuable books, whole libraries were thrown from the balconies into the streets. It was an example of direct and ferocious justice in the hands of those who had suffered the horrors of the dictatorship.

The lootings and physical violence did not last long, but armed students, going through the confidential archives of the Police Department, continued to seize killers and informers, some of whom were executed without trial. In the country's interior the sugar-cane workers occupied the sugar mills, most of which were American property. The hunger and exploitation of the five-cent day could no longer be accepted.

The new President, Céspedes, was neutral; there was nothing either for or against him. He had never been involved in Cuban public life, had lived mostly abroad, holding a diplomatic post, and was even married to a foreigner. When he had been in office twenty-three days without inspiring the least popular enthusiasm or undertaking any project whatsoever for the alleviation of the country's distress, the Cuban people awoke one morning—September 4, 1933—to an unexpected news bulletin: the President had been deposed.

The sergeants and soldiers of the army and the enlisted men of the navy had struck, and had relieved their officers of their commands. The Student Directorate and a sergeant named Batista spoke on the radio announcing the *fait accompli*. The student leaders had been called to the Columbia Military Camp to participate in the formation of a Civil Junta. Everything connected with mediation was swept away. We were going to have what Mr. Welles and the officers who had helped Machado to flee had tried to prevent. We were going to have the renewal of Cuba, sanctions against the late dictatorship's wrongdoers, improved conditions for labor, autonomy for the university, freedom and equal rights for all.

Those were colorful days, and their events are difficult to narrate in an orderly, consecutive way. One thing I remember clearly. Pablo, who at the first hint of Machado's fall had rushed back from his exile in the United States, took me to visit the presidential palace, which had been thrown open to all after the deposition of Céspedes. Forty-eight hours after that second coup, hundreds of students were still walking through the building, going in and out of the rooms as if they were walking about in their own houses. Pablo went off to another part of the palace to report a committee meeting, and I went wandering through the building. A polite soldier accompanied me as I investigated here and there—Machado's bedroom, his huge bathroom, the kitchen . . .

As we crossed a corridor next to the presidential chambers, I saw two small Louis XV sofas, and in them, incongruously, two sergeants, one navy and one army, curled up and sound asleep. The latter was disheveled and very thin, with sunken cheeks and a look of utter exhaustion. It was Fulgencio Batista. The other was the new navy chief. I recalled having seen Batista once before, during Machado's time, when civilians were tried by military tribunals. A very dear friend of Pablo's— Pablo was in the Isle of Pines Penitentiary at the time— was being tried, and after one of the hearings, his fiancée and I had approached that thin sergeant who was the court stenographer and who had from time to time thrown us a look of sympathy, and had asked him if her fiancé was all right. Batista had reassured her, saying that he would probably not be condemned to death. (He was right; the prisoner was given thirty years and sent to the Isle of Pines.)

"He's the one who pulled it off," the soldier told me, indicating Batista. "He's getting his first sleep in three days."

The young students did not know what to do with their new power. They had not dreamed of such a situation. Now it was for them to give Cuba a government. After many hours without sleep, after deliberations and more deliberations, they decided to institute a pentarchy, with each of the five representing a sector of the population that had contributed to the struggle against Machado. The Communists, very unpopular since their back-to-work order during the general strike, were not invited to participate.

The pentarchy was composed of two university professors, a newspaper editor, an independent and unsullied politician, and an old banker of a respectable family in Havana society. The Student Directorate held no posts but was consulted by the pentarchy on all issues. The student mass of Cuba was going to be the government's principal support. Raúl Roa, one of the student leaders at the time, and today the Minister of Foreign Affairs in Fidel Castro's government, called it the "ephebocracy," or teen-aged government. Students of all ages poured into the offices of the government ministries. To avoid a repetition of the violence that had followed the fall of the dictator, committees were formed for the expurgation of *Machadistas*. A Tribunal of Sanctions was appointed to investigate and prosecute the guilty.

During the general strike the workers of the Half Moon and Mabay sugar mills had taken over their mills and demanded minimum wages and hours, the right to organize and strike, etc.—all those demands for workers' rights are an accepted fact in any democratic society. Under the pentarchy they were still occupying the mills, refusing to budge until their rights were granted. The whole island, moreover, continued to erupt in strikes, making similar demands. Trying to arrange matters, the members of the Student Directorate rushed off to all parts of the country to listen to the demands and transmit them to the government. Both the students and the pentarchy had their hands full, and it was too much for them. Too much was happening.

The pentarchy lasted six days. As a governing body it was too miscellaneous to be effective. Cuba was in turmoil, and there were too many diverse figures and groups to deal with, each of whom was a force in the country. There were the embattled sugar-mill workers. There were the aroused city workers. There were the deposed army and navy officers. There were the Rightists, favoring the of-

64

ficers, and the Leftists, favoring the workers. There was the pro-democratic, anti-colonial temper of the times, represented by the students and intellectuals. There was Batista, representing the army, acclaimed by the people because he had deposed Machado's officers. And there was Sumner Welles, "the Gentleman from Virginia," representing the United States and its interests.

Welles was indignant at the upsetting of his plans and declared a personal, private war against Batista that lasted several months and that was to end only with his recall. His first move materialized on September 5, the day after the sergeant's coup, when units of the U.S. fleet entered Havana Bay.

In spite of the apparent imminence of a marine landing, this time the Cubans were not frightened. The population of Havana poured out on the quay shouting "Get out! Go back to your country! You have no business here!" An unidentified Cuban took out his revolver and fired a shot at one of the battleships. The gesture was ridiculous but symbolic, and was much commented on in the newspapers and in the streets. I was present, though I hardly know how I got there or with whom. (Already I was rushing around everywhere, gathering items for Pablo's news reports.)

To Roosevelt's credit, there was no landing of the marines, and Cuban blood was not shed by Americans. Welles, on the other hand, was directly involved in its being shed by Cubans. Just as he had engineered the fall of Machado—who obviously would have fallen without him—he now set about trying to engineer the fall of the revolutionary government and of Batista, who was still at that point resting unambitiously in the background, content with having been given the rank of colonel and named Chief of the Armed Forces. On September 9 the dismissed officers moved into the Hotel Nacional, where the Ambassador was living, and began holding confer-

65

ences with Mr. Welles and his military attaché, while the hotel converted itself into an armed fortress.

On September 10, six days after its inception, the unhappy pentarchy was dissolved and Ramón Grau San Martín, one of the two university professors and the only one of the five the Student Directorate had been able to keep at his post, was proclaimed President. It was hoped this would stimulate recognition by the other governments, but only Mexico continued formal relations. The foreign diplomatic corps, waiting to see what position the United States took with respect to recognition, did not attend the ceremony at which Dr. Grau was installed as President. U.S. recognition would not come until several months later, and not while Sumner Welles was there and Batista was not yet a tyrant.

With the country in a state of anarchy after the September 4 coup, military control had to be exercised over the whole island, and from the first, Batista demonstrated an ability to organize and command. The new army began to establish a corps of high-ranking officers, taken from among the soldiers, corporals and sergeants—an improvised caste that would treat Cuba with true barbarity for many years.

In November, Batista government forces attacked the Hotel Nacional when the ex-officers refused to quit their new headquarters. The Special Ambassador had moved out by then because of the pointed commentaries and because he knew a battle was looming. Years later tourists visiting Havana could still see the scars on the walls of the hotel which, exposed on all sides, came under the concentrated fire of Batista's gunboats. At the same time there was an uprising by the ABC, a fascist terrorist organization left over from the time of Machado and supporting Welles and the ex-officers. The ABC staged its uprising in Havana and also attacked barracks and fortresses, and filled Havana with snipers firing from the rooftops at the soldiers maintaining order. The uprising took over a thousand lives, and was put down by the new army of Batista with the help of the students.

The first government of Grau San Martín, coming as it did in the wake of a dictatorship that had left the country in economic chaos, could not avoid the troubles and turbulence that rose to meet it. His four months in office were characterized by agitation and strikes all over the island and by war between Right and Left in the student and worker camps. It was Cuba's first nationalist government. The Communist Party, being an internationalist organization, fought tooth and nail against every one of the nationalist decrees issued by Grau and his governing secretary, Antonio Guiteras, who was the real force behind Grau. The Communists were not interested in the problem of Cuba per se; they called all nationalistic governments "chauvinistic."

The Grau-Guiteras administration made many mistakes and had many inherent faults, but it established laws to protect the Cuban worker, pressed for repeal of the Platt Amendment, and took measures which, though they flaunted the American interests, were vitally necessary for the stabilization of the Cuban economy. The Law of Fifty Per Cent, or the Labor Nationalization Law, required at least half of Cuba's labor force to be Cuban by birth or naturalization. Another law provided for the improvement of workers' conditions. This was followed by a decree repudiating the payments of interest and the debt of $80 million that Machado had contracted with the Chase National Bank for the realization of a public-works program. The loan was repudiated on the grounds that it was illegally made by an illegal Congress and in spite of the fact that the bank was well aware of Cuba's unsettled financial and political state under Machado. Of course the Chase had placed the bonds of that loan among the American population, and the repudiation was hurting many people in America. (Indisputably the government of the United States must demand a greater sense of responsibility from its banks in their international dealings and investments, especially in negotiations with tyrants. Behind these tyrants will always come those who will be unwilling to acknowledge the illegal debts thrust upon a whole people. Two months before Machado fell, incidentally, Cuba had a total debt of almost $165 million, of which only $7,816,000 was an interior debt. We had, besides, a floating debt of $50 million.)

In November the Battle of the Hotel Nacional and the uprising of the ABC had taken place. On November 24, 1933, Sumner Welles was called back to the United States, and on December 18 Jefferson Caffery arrived in Havana as President Roosevelt's personal representative. An evil reputation preceded him.

Caffery was the Machiavelli who transformed the ex-sergeant from a humble man of the people with compelling oratorical emotionality and, at the beginning, no desire for personal aggrandizement or honors, into a brutal "strong man." Instead of opposing Batista as Welles had done, he sought his friendship, and his siren songs softened the ear of the thin little sergeant-turned-colonel whose wife was a laundress (and a good woman whom nobody ever disliked). Every morning Caffery went to the Columbia Army Camp where Batista lived and took him riding, practicing his horsemanship and conversing with him in the friendliest fashion; or they would go on a visit to the Jesuit fathers at the school of Belen, for Caffery was a recent convert to Roman Catholicism. Batista (unlike Fidel Castro) always liked the company of better informed people and listened to their advice. He was still humble then, and was adapting himself to a new environment.

Meanwhile, the nationalistic program of the Grau government continued, irritating not only the Americans but Batista, who desperately wanted American recognition and who was, moreover, rapidly coming under the influence of his new friend. The government expropriated two sugar mills of American ownership and nationalized them. But what actually brought about the fall of that government was the attempt to reduce the cost of electricity, which was such a vitally necessary measure. The Cuban Electric Company was a subsidiary of Electric Bond & Share, which charged its offshoot high prices for materials and honorary consultations, and demanded high wages for its executives, who, before the Labor Nationalization Law, were always Americans. The Cuban Electric Company, which had already defied and been forced to comply with the Grau government's labor laws improving the workers' conditions, now defied its order to reduce the cost of electricity, whereupon the government took over the electric plants. That occurred on January 14, 1934. On January 15 the government fell. Batista, who had been clashing more and more frequently with Guiteras, compelled Grau to offer his resignation, which, after an agitated meeting with the students of the Directorate, was accepted.

Batista wished to install a candidate favored by the Americans, Carlos Mendieta. A compromise was effected whereby Carlos Hevia, an engineer and a moderate man politically, was made President, but after thirty-eight hours Batista removed him and replaced him with Mendieta. Within six days the Mendieta government had won American recognition, the denial of which had contributed so greatly to the Grau government's instability. (A little over a year later Batista had Guiteras murdered in an ambush.)

With Mendieta came the end of the revolutionary government, a government that had been doomed from the outset because of its lack of political cohesion and of a definite program. And so Cuba fell into the hands of "the

Strong Man of Columbia," whose method of achieving power was the *coup d'état,* and whose method of keeping it was based on military strength. In future he would install and remove presidents at will, while he alone did the governing. He already knew how to get rid of his enemies. One of his first victims was Mario Hernández, an important conspirator in the September 4 coup against the officers. That coup had in reality been prepared not by Batista but by other sergeants whom he was able to dominate by virtue of his being a stenographer and thus, in the eyes of the conspirators, something of an "intellectual." The "intellectual" now had an able mentor in Caffery, who in those early days was a factor in every development. The installation of Mendieta as President was Caffery's doing, and the recognition which immediately followed converted Caffery from special envoy to ambassador. He was the first American envoy to Cuba ever to need bodyguards.

Under Mendieta the strikes and confusion continued, and the hard hand of the Batista-directed government grew harder still. Machine guns were trained on the rebellious sugar mills. In Mabay they fired at the workers. Imprisoned students were murdered in cold blood. As in the time of Machado, the army began to shove civilians around, to knock people down, to make arbitrary arrests, and, together with the police, to kill.

It was in that turbulent epoch that I matriculated at the university, which had been reopened by the revolutionary government. But the oldest student demand, university autonomy, had still not been granted, and we knew that in the current state of upheaval it was only a matter of time before the institution was again occupied militarily and converted into a barracks, as it had been by Machado. In the perpetual assemblies held by the students I began to be a leader. One day, late in the afternoon, we—the university leaders—were informed that the university was going to be taken over by the police. We decided not to leave. We had no arms, but they would have to kill us all if they tried to occupy our alma mater. We were about twenty. Armed soldiers and policemen surrounded the university, which stands on a hill, and fired tear-gas shells at us from the nearest roofs. We held out by tying handkerchiefs soaked in vinegar over our noses like masks. Pablo heard of what was happening and came rushing over to share whatever fate was in store for us, to protect me, as he always did in his lifetime. He sprinted between two soldiers and came racing up the great stairway, over a hundred meters high, and reached us safely, gasping, "Where is Teté?" It is a marvel that he was not shot. I think it was surprise, plus the fact that the soldiers and police thought the university was stacked with arms and ammunition—which was not true—that held them back.

All Havana was agitated that evening. Newspaper editors, public figures, cabinet ministers tried to solve the crisis and avoid more bloodshed. Just before midnight the troops were withdrawn. We had won the battle. But knowing they might return at any moment, we organized a university strike demanding the protection of autonomy. We students still had much national strength, and when we threatened to extend the strike to schools throughout the island, the government decided to give in to our demand. I was the only girl among the seven or eight members of the strike committee. Eight thousand students, who in general assembly had elected us to bring our ultimatum to the presidential palace, declared themselves in permanent session and waited for our return.

We set out for the presidential palace, and against our expectations we were attended to and received as if we were ambassadors. Mendieta evidently wanted to smooth things over. He came to greet us in person, was very attentive, and conducted us to the Cabinet Room, where

71

he invited us to sit around a long table which he presided over. As the only lady present, I was seated at the opposite end. He asked us why we were so anxious to have autonomy. We gave him our reasons. But all this was pure formality, because he opened a drawer and took out a roll of parchment on which was written the presidential decree granting autonomy to the University of Havana. It was to me that he handed it, so that I should be the one who carried and presented it to the student body. He very courteously saw us out and we left in a state of joyful astonishment, trying to hide our emotion and particularly our surprise. We had had no idea that the decree had already been prepared for that eventuality.

I think that that has been for me the most solemn and important occasion of my life. During the automobile ride from the palace to the university I held that scroll in my hand as if I were carrying the sacred fire of a beautiful temple. What I was carrying represented a twelve-year struggle that began with Julio Antonio Mella; a struggle during the course of which many dear friends died, like Mella, without seeing the victory; I repeated their names to myself; I felt as if I were a little girl again, leaving church after receiving Holy Communion. Suddenly I became aware that the boys were getting out. We had arrived before the amphitheater; a group came toward me while everybody announced to everybody else: "Teté is bringing the Decree of Autonomy!" Protecting the scroll, I raised my arm high. Now many close companions surrounded me, Leftists and Rightists alike, shouting enthusiastically with the popular "Fatty" Saavedra at their head, and pulling me out of the car—to carry me on their shoulders! Thus did I enter the amphitheater that unforgettable morning, carried past my eight thousand comrades. They finally stood me on a large table on the dais. After prolonged applause and happy laughter, and shouts, and cheers, someone made the announcement that I was going to read the document. Instantly the silence was so profound that the reading resembled a religious ceremony. With what pride did I read that document that meant so much to us! It was the most truly radiant morning of my life.

The newly autonomous university decided on a school government made up equally of professors and students. As a member of the Governing Council, my first act was to ask for a salary raise for the ushers, who had always stood by us in our gravest crises. I also put through a total reform of the plan of studies for the antiquated pedagogy course, and supported the Left Wing proposal instituting free matriculation for students of insufficient means. Another measure that was put through, and that I opposed, enabled the large student body to make up for the three lost years by shortening the normally nine-month courses to four months, and these to run consecutively, without intermediate vacations. Under this new arrangement, I went through in one year.

Even so, Pablo could not wait until I got out of the university to marry me, and we were married while still students. It was a lovely church wedding in a hermitage situated on top of a hill. My immense veil of white tulle was like a cloud. Our friends lined up along the slope of the hill and threw rice and shouted cheers and congratulations. We had a beautiful little apartment . . . in which we spent just one month of our hazardous marital life. After that we were in constant flight from the police and had to sleep in the houses of friends like escaped prisoners.

Autonomy protected the university, but it did not protect the Cuban people, nor did it protect us outside the university grounds. Every day some one or other of our companions was killed. We never knew who might be the next to fall. I confess there were times when I had an intimate knowledge of what fear is. To descend that long flight of steps from the university with the determination of running through a few streets shouting protests and trying to get as far as the Central Park for a public meeting we knew would end under a hail of bullets was something to shrink one's stomach. We called them "hit and run meetings." Often the gunfire would be waiting to receive us at the foot of the steps. No, it was not easy to concentrate on one's studies in 1934, 1935. . . . I would go home, to wherever we were staying at the time, without knowing where my husband was, and sit down with a textbook to study for examinations. I remember that one day I got home to study for an examination in biology after a very dear friend, like Pablo and myself, recently married and happy, had been killed not half an hour after we had stood talking on the university steps. I opened the book and read a sentence of Claude Bernard's: "Death is a phenomenon of perfection." My eyes still filled with the image of my friend's corpse as it had been carried still warm to the university hospital, I threw the book from me violently. Our comrade's death was a phenomenon of absurdity! He had been gentle, intelligent, useful, loved, full of life and illusions. What perfection could his death hold? What did the science of all that stuff know?

For days I rebelled against books, against life, against everything in a protest of pure pain against all those who were persecuting us simply because we asked them to stop killing citizens and filling the jails with the best of Cuba's people—intellectuals, labor leaders, and all who had joined the students in their fight for freedom and civil rights.

By the time I took my last examination the atmosphere in the whole country was so tense, and so ferocious had the dictatorship of Batista become, that any attempts at concerted action had to be organized in the university. It was the only place where gatherings could be held without

74

police interference. And so it was there that the general strike of March 1935 was plotted and organized.

It was a revolutionary strike, but was not accompanied by any armed uprisings. All Cuba and even the government employees responded to the call of the university students. For nine days the whole country was paralyzed. On the seventh day, with the entire population involved in the strike and everything at a standstill, the cities without light, without transport, without movement, Batista decided to flee. He informed his friend and patron, Jefferson Caffery, of his intention, and Caffery hurried to the palace, where he found Batista meeting with his closest collaborators, ready to announce his decision. Roundly opposed to this decision, the Ambassador prevailed upon the dictator to resist the strike and crush it. But Batista did not want to assume that responsibility. It was Eleuterio Pedraza, Chief of the Havana police, who assumed it. And so it came about that Cuba was bathed in blood, and that a newly consolidated dictatorship was able to last another ten years.

The strike collapsed in its eleventh day. It is impossible to recount in full the terror of those black days of unleashed barbarity, and I will cite only two cases: One day during the strike we sent a representative to attend a secret meeting being held by a group of workers in a building on a street named Someruelos. He was our link with this group. The boy returned as pale as a corpse, and as speechless. When he was able to speak, he told us that he had arrived at the address and, seeing no one about, had gone up to the apartment. The door was open, so he went inside, only to find the apartment empty, but with so much blood on the floors that the youth shuddered to remember it. He said it was "as if buckets of blood had been poured over those floors." We never knew how many people had died there.

One very popular and beloved student, Armando Feito,

had fought against Machado, but had since retired from political activity after his marriage and the birth of a child. One day during the strike the police went to his home, in search of victims. All of us involved in the movement had left off living in our own houses, and as almost none of the desired conspirators had been found, the police selected Feito as a sacrificial alternate because of his earlier activities. They told him he was under arrest, and when his wife showed concern, his father-in-law, a man of seventy, offered to accompany him to the police station. Two hours later their bodies were found in a park in Havana, horribly mutilated, their hands tied with wire.

Human life was cheap in those last panic-filled days of the March strike, when the better part of a generation was liquidated and the remainder dispersed. The ruthless suppression, the collapse of the strike, the closing of the university made it pointless for the more active and known among us to stay, and the survivors of that Generation of the Thirties fled to Mexico and the United States. Pablo, whose written denunciations of the regime's policy of government by assassination had made him one of the special targets of the police, refused to go. He did not leave until he himself saw that, for the time being, there was nothing to be done in Cuba. He was one of the last to go.

chapter

5

"... And I could find nothing to lay my eyes on that was not a reminder of death." With these words borrowed from a Spanish classic, I could sum up the next twenty years of my life, the twenty years that passed between the collapse of the general strike of March 1935 and my meeting Fidel Castro. I lived those years like a ghostly survivor of the brilliant generation of students that Cuba and its university produced in the thirties, a generation that came to an untimely end, as a unified force, in the March strike. Henceforth it was to be an "absent" generation, as whoever remained alive went wandering through life like one removed from everything around him. When I wrote my first novel, *The Absent,* eight years later, I began it with the above quotation. The writing of that book represented the first time in my life that I consciously made myself stop and look back on the past, and it did me much harm. After having been swept along by life, as by a hurricane lashing at one from all directions, one can no longer look anywhere but ahead. And, though I have grown used to saying good-by to people and to dreams, it is still hard for me, even now, to look back on those twenty years of being one of the absent.

In New York, though in exile and quite poor, Pablo and I were able for the first time to be together in an atmosphere of peace. It was there that we had our real honeymoon. But our life was not easy. Pablo worked at anything he could find. He worked in factories, restaurants, and at the same time sent articles to newspapers and magazines in different Latin American countries. He wrote the articles at night, when he came home dropping with fatigue and with his feet inflamed after eleven hours of continuous work. He did not want us to live on what my parents sent to help us out, nor did he want me to work. I insisted on trying it, however, and was dismissed from two factories for not fulfilling the requirements. I learned what it is to be a common laborer. I worked long hours for low pay, having a sandwich inside the factory at lunchtime to avoid eating standing up in some disagreeable and crowded cafeteria. It was dark when I left home and dark again when I returned. The day I received my second dismissal I climbed jubilantly out of the subway to the surface of the city eager to enjoy the sunshine and to watch the first birds of spring. Shortly thereafter I matriculated at Columbia University for a course of language instruction, where I made several fine friendships, and we founded a club for exiles, calling it the "José Martí Club." We gathered there to study, hold meetings, prepare the newspaper which we sent secretly to Cuba, and warm ourselves in the familiar, comradely atmosphere of compatriots. Although never poorer, I think I have never been more content or in better company.

In Cuba the regime of dictatorship consolidated itself in silence, in terror, in crowded jails. The ex-sergeant rose from colonel to general. He made and removed two more presidents. He was the absolute ruler of the country and of his army, which he showered with privileges while increasing its strength from ten to eighteen thousand men. By 1936 that peace and quiet which had been so ardently desired by the investors and by the American Ambassador had been attained. It was the peace of the absent and the quiet of the dead. Batista believed that the energy to resist was exhausted, and, as was the custom in Cuba when elections were going to be held and pacification was desired, he offered a general amnesty. When he had installed a new president and a new Congress, he reopened the university, which had remained closed after the strike. The weary exiles began making plans to return. Of course the return would have to be effected in a mood of submission—silently and with acceptance of the status quo that had been imposed by the new ruling caste, the army. Naturally the press would continue to be closely watched and controlled. Pablo did not care to return under those conditions. Events quickly proved him right: almost immediately the new President, Miguel Mariano Gómez, was set upon by Batista's puppet Congress.

Then, in July, the Spanish Civil War broke out, and that was where Pablo went. He left New York in August, and I returned to Cuba to stay with my parents until he sent for me. In his first letter from Spain, however, he wrote that it was no place for me, and I must not think of going there for the time being. He had gone as a reporter, planning to send his chronicles to Mexico and South America via a friend in New York. (Their publication in Batista's pro-Franco Cuba, of course, was out of the question.) But in November, Hitler's air force bombed Madrid ferociously, and Pablo, who wrote me continually although he had no rest in his reportorial labors, described those bombings and added: "I cannot stay seated before a typewriter while the city is being bombed. I go out into the street and see the mangled bodies of women, children, beasts of burden. . . . On the radio two women, 'La Pasionaria' and Margarita Nelken, are calling pathetically for all able-bodied men to take up rifles and help defend Madrid. I am going to offer myself as a volunteer. I will fight beside the Spaniards. When the danger is past, I will return to my typewriter."

I learned of his death on the Madrid front in a newspaper. He died fighting with a Spanish brigade led by the popular peasant "El Campesino." On the fall of the Republic, his remains were carried out by a retreating Cuban, but they have never since been located, and Pablo, like Ignacio Agramonte, of whom he used to tell me when he was a youth of seventeen and I a fascinated girl of seven, has no known grave.

The only thing left for me to do after his death, I felt, was to have his writings on Spain published. While waiting for his chronicles to be sent to me from New York, I determined to do something to help the unhappy people for whose liberty Pablo had given his life. Accordingly, I founded the Association for Assistance to the Children of Spain, the only organization for Spanish aid not banned by Batista. The organization's membership grew to 300,000, with a delegation in every town on the island, and the amount of assistance we gave to the Spanish people was enormous. We sent frequent boatloads of food and established on the beach at Sitges, in Catalonia, a children's shelter which we maintained up to the end of the war. For seven months I worked hard building up this organization, speaking over the air and at meetings, visiting villages all over the island, helping to get out our monthly publication, soliciting co-operation through magazine and newspaper articles. Then I went to Mexico to arrange the publication of Pablo's war chronicles. I went for three months, and stayed almost two years.

My project to get the chronicles published was held up by the Communists. Pablo's friend in New York, who was to have sent the chronicles on to Mexican and South American editors, had given them to the Communist Party instead, which tried to keep me from having them because the collection was going to include a foreword by Raúl Roa. Roa was one of Pablo's most devoted friends and, until very recently, an irreconcilable enemy of the

Communist Party. Another friend came to my aid. This was Juan Marinello, a poet and intellectual who had been with Pablo in the Isle of Pines Prison, and who was president of the Cuban Popular Socialist (communist) Party at the time. The chronicles were finally sent to me in Mexico, after a long delay, and I was able to have them published.

In Mexico, while I was waiting for the chronicles to arrive from New York, I met an aspiring film director who gave me the feminine lead in his first picture. It came about quite by accident. I met him at the League of Writers and Artists; he thought me photogenic, gave me a screen test, and suddenly I was an actress. I did another picture and then, in 1938, married a Mexican writer who shortly afterward entered the diplomatic corps. As I greatly longed for my parents, he arranged to be stationed in Cuba and we went there in 1939, arriving, by a sad coincidence, on the day the Spanish Civil War ended. Havana was greatly changed. I had little desire to visit the university. I went there only twice. It was a different place from the one I had known, and for me full of the ghosts of dead friends. As often happens after a turbulent period, the revolutionary agitations of Cuba and the university had been followed by a vacuum, by the quiet of exhaustion and forgetfulness, and by a demoralized, conservative state of mind. The valiant, unarmed young men of the early thirties had been succeeded by groups of student gangsters. With the authority of the pistol they took over the university and the secondary schools. Pablo's friend Ramiro Valdés Daussá, at whose trial I had met Batista, was murdered by a university gang when as a professor in the School of Engineering he had tried to bring the student hoodlums into line. They were not brought to justice for their crime. Batista made it easy for such killers to flee the country.

In 1939 the Communists made peace, and a pact, with

Batista. Ironically, the political support which they had withheld from the man at the beginning when he had been a popular figure they gave him when he became dictator. In 1940, by means of an "election" influenced by the presence of the army, Batista had himself installed in the President's chair, and the Communist Party took power with him, placing ministers, representatives, and senators in his government.

The about-face agility of the Communists was not new to me. I had seen it operating in my university days, when the students were split into Left and Right Wing groups. Neither Pablo nor I was ever a member of the Communist Party, but we belonged to the Left Wing because it fought for the poor students and for the economic liberation of Cuba. I joined the Left Wing on the day one of its leaders, Gabriel Barceló, recounted in a clear, informative, and convincing way, before an assembly of university students, the colonial tragedy of a Cuba oppressed by imperialism. Never before had such things been mentioned in the schools. There were, of course, Communists among the Left Wingers, and both Pablo and I were able to observe the Communist mentality in action. We saw how in the name of the Left Wing, of which they were only a fraction, they continually provoked and attacked the Right Wing in an attempt to achieve their ends, one of which was to take control of the entire student body. On one occasion I was instrumental in preventing a physical clash between the two wings in the university square by making it clear, in a voice for all to hear, that I was not in agreement with the unjust accusations leveled at the Right Wing. The Communist segment never forgave me, and referred to me sarcastically as "the perfumed bourgeoise," but thereafter, with the exception of the sincere and respected Barceló and one or two others, it was they, the Communists, who were whistled back into their seats when they rose to speak at our assemblies. (Raúl Roa called me, mockingly, "the Left Wing Frances of Assisi.") So I began early to see what the Communists were. Any of their number who reasoned things out for themselves in an understanding, undogmatic way were condemned by their comrades and expelled from the Party. I saw them crucify good, valuable people like Barceló, who gave his health to their cause, and who died soon after that memorable assembly—at which his talk had moved so many students—beset and censured by his own comrades. And I saw them crucify, too, Rubén Martínez Villena, the founder of the Cuban Communist Party, who was a fine poet and a dear friend of Pablo's, by throwing all the blame on him for that back-to-work order during the general strike against Machado in 1933, he had given his whole life to the Party, and his "comrades" hastened his death from tuberculosis by harassing him with attacks that were as unjust as they were cruel.

After witnessing such things, I began to see that that generosity, that Christian brotherhood which I had attributed to the Communist idea—because such was Rubén —was in reality riddled with vindictiveness and envy and baseness; that it was the offended ones, those who felt in some way frustrated, racially or otherwise, who sought refuge in the Communist Party, which act did not necessarily help them to surmount their resentment and become true comrades. They behaved like dehumanized men, like automatons geared to destroy but helpless to construct. It was my first political disillusionment. Years later I was to have the same experience with Fidel Castro, who veered toward the Communists because, resentful and obsessed with destruction and with a sense of guilt that weighed heavily on his mind, that was where he fit in. I also saw them throw a Puerto Rican named Juan Juarbe (now Cuban delegate to the U.N.!) out of a Cultural Congress bodily, calling him "filthy Trotskyite," when he rose to speak against North American imperialism. The reason? It was during World War II, and they were then the allies of the United States, and of Batista. For the Communist Party, during the war, the phenomenon of imperialism no longer existed; the very word was taboo.

Yet the alliance between Batista and the Communists could have been foreseen, if the hand were not quicker than the eye, as far back as 1933, when the latter sabotaged the nationalistic, anti-imperialistic program of Grau and Guiteras at every turn. Guiteras' two bitterest foes, because of that program, were the future allies, Batista and the Communist Party. But despite my having grown accustomed to their ways, I thought the Communists were exaggerating the spirit of their 1939 alliance with Batista when they published Pedraza's portrait in the Party newspaper, *Hoy,* congratulating him on his name day with the caption, "A correct and gentlemanly friend, the Chief of the Havana Police." I took the trouble to visit the newspaper's office and to remind its editors of their many comrades who had been vilely assassinated by Pedraza's police in the general strike of March 1935.

Batista too, in 1940, was eager to forget the past, in hopes that the Cuban people would follow suit. Having given an aura of legality to the perpetuity of his supreme command by making himself President, he now tried to draw a veil over the bloody phase of his rule by holding popular elections for a Constituent Assembly. The elected Assembly then drew up the free and advanced "Constitution of 1940," which established citizens' rights and protection for workers and farmers—all the things we had so bitterly fought for in our earlier struggle. In 1944, when Batista wished to go off safely and enjoy the great fortune he had amassed in his ten years of power, he performed the cleverest of all his maneuvers: he permitted honest elections, in which his candidate was over-whelmingly defeated. The victor was Grau San Martín, who since that first turbulent term as President had become a popular figure in Cuba, despite the fact that the one who had been responsible for that administration's popular measures was, as I have said, Antonio Guiteras. In any case, the overwhelming vote in Grau's favor was not so much for him, really, as it was against Batista's candidate.

Grau, in his second term, was one of the very worst presidents we have ever had. He fomented group warfare by setting the student gangs against each other. Corruption spread throughout the island. Sugar was bringing a high price at that time, and the pockets of the government officials filled with plunder. The country fell into one of its most shameful states in our history. The people, weary of dying in the endless struggles against Machado and Batista, now went to the opposite extreme, wanting only to live well, no matter by what means.

The only good thing that can be said about the second Grau administration is that the beneficent labor legislation initiated by the Constituent Assembly in 1940 was not impeded in its progress to becoming the most advanced in Latin America.

My husband and I had divorced in 1944, just before Grau's inauguration, and I had left once again for Mexico. We parted amicably and have continued to have an affectionate regard for each other. I returned to Mexico because my novel, *The Absent,* had been chosen to represent Cuba in a Latin American novel competition and the wartime scarcity of paper in Cuba made it necessary to publish the book there; I could also support myself by working in the Mexican film industry. Except for brief trips, I stayed in that country through the next fifteen years.

The character of the Mexican film industry had

changed. It was Big Business now, and no longer appealed
to me as it once had. My career as an actress finally ended
after four more pictures, when a producer who was interviewing me on the subject of a part in his next picture
suggested we go away for a weekend together. I went to
work for a newspaper instead, and did not set foot in a
film studio again unless it was on a journalistic assignment. I earned much less, but felt much better. Thus I
was a reporter when in 1948 the President-elect of Cuba,
Carlos Prío Socarrás, came to Mexico. To my astonishment, for we had not seen each other in years, he sent the
Cuban Ambassador to bring me to his official residence in
Chapultepec Castle. He was the same cordial companion
who had been so fond of Pablo and so good a friend to me
in that distant and wonderful past when, with things
relatively quiet, a small group of us would sing songs and
recite poetry in the shade of the ancient trees in the university's Patio of Laurels. He was still the gentle, sensi-
tive friend who had understood that when Pablo had
died he had made me more than a widow: I was an
orphan. Before I left, Carlos told me he would send me an
invitation to come to Cuba for his inauguration. I did
not think he would remember, but when the inauguration date was near, I received a return-trip ticket to Cuba
and an invitation to the official ceremonies. I could not
go, for two reasons. The first was that my springer spaniel
Menina, who was then still a puppy, was desperately ill
with distemper. My second reason lay on the mantelpiece
beside the Prío invitation: it was a notice of eviction. A
shortage of funds had obliged the newspaper I worked for
to reduce its staff, beginning with the aliens, and I had
fallen three months behind in the rent. I had put the
Prío communication beside the eviction notice as a
beacon against despair. And whoever does not believe in
miracles, let him laugh at me; for I have seen them occur.
That interminable night Menina came safely through her

crisis despite the veterinarian's prediction that she would die. And the next afternoon, at six o'clock, a film producer came to my house and said he needed a complete screen play on a bull-fighting theme within twenty-four hours, in order to sign a contract the next day with Luis Procuna, the famous matador. I went to work and, the following afternoon, handed him the screen play and received a check that enabled me to pay all my debts.

Once again my life entered upon one of its "ascendant phases." A month after Prío's inauguration I went to Cuba with that gift passage. But I was unwilling to live in the Cuba that was now permeated with politics, and Carlos, who had wanted me to stay, gave me a post in our embassy in Mexico. He appointed me commercial attaché, a position which carned the highest salary after that of the ambassador. Commerce between our two countries was practically non-existent, however, and my work in Mexico was actually that of cultural attaché. In 1950 I was a member of the Cuban delegation to the General Conference of UNESCO, and traveled for several months through various European countries. With the proceeds of a book based on recollections of that trip, I bought my first automobile and took my parents on an extensive tour of Mexico. Then, shortly after their return to Cuba, Batista's *coup d'état* of March 10, 1952, overthrew the constitutional government, and I was again out of a job.

Batista, as I have mentioned, did not actually prepare his coups. He stole them. In this second one he arrived at the Columbia Military Camp after the others had got everything ready; cleverer and more experienced than they, he was soon able to take over command of the coup and of Cuba. The United States immediately recognized Batista—who, like Franco in Spain, set himself up as Chief of State—despite the fact that the deposed government of Prío had been an absolutely democratic one. At that time U.S. foreign policy was still more interested in "friends" than in true democracy. It was the era of "strong men." Batista's example spread like a contagion throughout Latin America, where military coups took place in several countries. Someone said of that period that the sickness of imperialism had suffered complications of "dictatoritis."

Though Prío had inherited the political turbulence and corruption of the Grau government, and though he received little support from the United States and none at all from the Communists, with whom he refused to make "deals," his term of office was a constructive one. He sponsored a series of good works and projects of a nationalistic nature, and when he was deposed, some few months before the expiration of his term, Cuba was gradually developing new industries and rescuing its national riches. He created the National Bank, which had long been an urgent necessity, and the Bank of Industrial and Agricultural Development, a useful and efficient organism intended to encourage economic development through careful study, technical orientation, and financial aid to new industries. Prío also satisfied an old popular demand by establishing an Accounts Tribunal for the recording and examining of all spending made by the State. It was one of his last measures and was in its organizational beginnings when his government was deposed. It is true that he made a large fortune while in office through speculations of a marginal nature. But he recognized his mistakes, and set up the machinery to put an end to administrative corruption. This would have eliminated a good many of the country's evils, but with the second advent of Batista, the Tribunal had no real chance to function. (The government of Fidel Castro reactivated it, but how is it possible to keep a check on officials who spend and spend without keeping books, and without having to account to anyone for the money invested? Indeed, Fidel Castro has recently announced the imminent abolition of that Tribunal, as part of his famous "for what?" refrain: "Judges, for what?" He once said, "Arms, for what?"—but then proceeded to convert Cuba into an arsenal of Russian weapons and "advisers," which *does* have for Cuba and for an uneasy Latin America a sinister "for what.")

The years between 1952 and 1956, when I met Fidel Castro, were strange ones for me. Although I was always busy doing something or other, my spirit sank into a kind of dreamy indolence. Perhaps it was because I was estranged from my country, removed from all political activity for the first time in my life; perhaps it was because my people were once again oppressed by a brutal tyranny they had lost all will to resist; but I retreated from the living world into a state of passivity and self-neglect, into a spiritual torpor that made memories of the past seem remote and unfamiliar, as if they belonged to some other woman. In those four years I worked on film scenarios and did translations for a living; I wrote two plays and another novel. When I was not working or writing I tried to occupy myself with reading, planting a lovely garden, taking courses on art and archeology, looking after my dogs. In a totally vacuous period I immersed myself in canasta and horse-racing, becoming an expert on thoroughbreds and even a columnist on the subject, until one day I came to my senses and left the beautiful Mexico City hippodrome for good. On that day, too, I stopped anesthetizing my evenings with mystery novels, and began reading philosophy, history, psychology. It was at about that time that one of my plays, *Utopia*, was being staged successfully. Yet my personal life continued to be burdened with a profound sense of inactivity and hopelessness.

My New Year's resolution for 1956 was to revive my spirits, fight for something, come back to life. I threw myself into the production and direction of another of my plays, whose first "angel" was my friend Adolfo López Mateos, who was to become President of Mexico. The play ran for two months in a high-cost, professional theater, and I broke even—a source of satisfaction for me to this day. The day it closed I received a donation from a distant "angel," Carlos Prío, with a very kind letter. "I envy you," he wrote, "because my lifelong dream was to be an actor, and if my dull wits had not brought me to the Presidency that is what I would have been."

I was beginning, slowly, to return to the living world, and when the play closed I decided I would write another novel I had in mind, and then move out of the house I had been living in since the embassy days. With its two stories, four bedrooms and huge garden, it required several servants and was expensive to maintain, and I was running out of money. When I finished the book, in July of 1956, I was behind in the rent.

To write that novel, I shut myself up in the house and disconnected myself from the outside world. I did not so much as look at a newspaper or turn on a radio. My cook, Tere (she was named Teresa, like myself, and was part Indian), brought me up a tray of food at noon and withdrew without speaking, and I went on writing. Often I wrote until late at night. When I did not it was because my house guest had come home particularly enthusiastic about the records she had brought back and wanted me to listen to them with her.

The house guest was a girl I will call Lilia. She was the daughter of a friend of mine who had left her with me in Mexico while she and her husband went on a cultural tour of the interior. Lilia has a great deal to do with this story and with the Fidel Castro I knew in Mexico.

Lilia was fresh and sprightly and extraordinarily beautiful. She was my great friend, and at the same time almost like a daughter, for I had known her in Cuba

90

when she was just two years old. Now she was eighteen, and she had everything—except temperament, as her mother, herself an exceptional woman, lamented. Lilia had been given an exceedingly polished and liberal education. Because of her beauty, disconcerting frankness, and an ingenuousness that enabled her to talk on every subject on earth, be it divine or mundane, she was pampered wherever she went. She was, naturally, familiar with classical music, a lover of Bach, Vivaldi, Mozart, but had a disconcerting weakness for popular songs that suffocated me. It was twenty years since I had heard such songs. Naturally they had delighted me too when I was her age, but I had never had the time or tranquillity to enjoy them. I had never even been to a dance. The time of my life in which I ought normally to have been learning such things I had spent among jails and student assemblies.

Lilia had been engaged, but had quarreled with her fiancé over the wedding plans and over his parents' objections to her lower social standing, and he had gone abroad. Every night she called me away from my typewriter to listen to the records she had brought back that afternoon from the music shop in which she worked. Gradually those nocturnal musical sessions together with Lilia's refined and genuine nature began reconverting me from the passionless mollusc I had become, looking on from the sidelines, into an active participant. We listened to Italian, French, and Mexican love songs of lovers' complaints and strummed guitars. Lilia talked about love, how delicious it was to receive the impassioned kiss of a man, to dance cheek to cheek. . . . I began to want to use make-up again, to wear high heels, to be a woman. Yielding to her insistence, I began to "modernize" myself, penciling my eyes in a certain way, and even let her teach me the mambo and the cha-cha-cha. I had begun my book with an epigraph quoting St. Theresa: "Hell is where there is no love." Now, as passion filtered into my novel and it became a song to the naturalness of living and loving, I found its title: *Welcome, Life!*

The book wrote itself, and on a Saturday morning in July it was done. I asked Tere to send out for a newspaper, which I read from top to bottom, including the advertisements. In an editorial I saw a reference to some young Cubans who were in the Mexico City Immigration Prison. A little less than a month ago they had been discovered on a ranch, training for an expedition which was intended to liberate Cuba from Batista. I smiled bitterly. The Cuban people, with pathetically few exceptions, had accepted in sorrow but in silence Batista's seizure of power. The Fighting Island was weary, disillusioned. Whatever remnant of hope it had left was mired in confusion, paralyzed by the general stupor.

That night Lilia had dined out with a young photographer friend of hers. When she returned, I told her I would like to communicate with those young Cuban prisoners, whose illusions, so remote from reality, touched me. I did not know if they were permitted visitors. She informed me that her friend was going to photograph them the following morning. Visiting hours were from twelve to two. She offered to accompany me. She was "bloody bored," she said, employing with delight one of her characteristically irreverent uses of the Spanish language.

When we arrived at the prison the next day, Lilia, whom I had been able to arouse from her profound, childlike slumber only by threatening to go alone, looked like an elegant model, with the rims of her enormous, innocent, greenish-brown eyes darkly accented in what she called the Italian fashion. On that day her hair was its natural color of dark gold. I, for my part, was for the first time in months dressed in my normal way.

More than fifty Cubans were gathered in the large central courtyard of the Immigration Prison. In the middle, tall and clean-shaven and with close-cropped chestnut hair, dressed soberly and correctly in a brown suit, standing out from the rest by his look and his bearing, was their chief, Fidel Castro. He gave one the impression of being noble, sure, deliberate—"like a big Newfoundland dog," as I later wrote in the first article to be published about him. He looked eminently serene, and inspired confidence and a sense of security. He gave me a greeting of restrained emotion, and a handshake that was warm without being overdone. His voice was quiet, his expression grave, his manner calm, gentle. I noticed he had a habit of shaking his head, like a fine thoroughbred horse. I introduced him to Lilia, who then went off to another part of the yard where the photographer was taking pictures.

Fidel began calling over his comrades and introducing them to me. Most of them knew of me and my past, largely through Pablo's writings or from what they had heard about us. Fidel was moved by my visit. No one not a member of the group, he said, had bothered to come or to concern himself about them. He said he felt deeply honored that I, with all I symbolized in Cuba, had come to see them. While introducing me to each member of his group, he shot sidelong glances from his superior height to where Lilia was standing. I smiled to myself as I realized that with all his gravity he reacted like any masculine young man to the charms of a beautiful girl. She, meanwhile, accustomed to the homage of the male sex, showed no sign of noticing his attention to her. An elderly Mexican woman came over to Fidel and hung a medallion around his neck. Another presented him with a cake. These were Gabriela and Alfonsina, humble, kind-hearted women who were like mothers to all the youths in exile.

My new friend took me off to a corner of the yard to introduce me to a companion who I instantly knew was intellectually the most impressive member of the group. It was Dr. Ernesto Guevara, whom most of the others called "The Doctor" and a few "El Che." He wore a heavy turtleneck sweater and was reading a thick medical book while sunning himself on that cold but brilliant morning. I had scarcely been introduced when his wife, a heavy woman with Indian features, arrived with their infant daughter. El Che raised the child in the air, playing with her like any father, then fell into conversation with his wife while Fidel and I drew away. Fidel told me she was Peruvian, and a member of APRA—a Peruvian political organization that had once had considerable strength, and that was anti-Communist as well as anti-imperialist. (El Che divorced her after the revolution and married the girl who had been his aide during its final phase.)

Finally we arrived beside Lilia, who was now cornered by a swarm of Cubans and a fascinated Canadian prisoner. They were telling her stories, jabbering, giving her their names. I walked away and was joined by others. All speaking at once, they told me how they had been caught, how they had been treated; they said two of their comrades had been taken away by the secret police and tortured for three days but had not "talked," and the police, impressed, had released them, and from then on had been treating their Cuban prisoners with respect. Considering the rest, I realized, with some disappointment, that with the exception of Che and Fidel these were humble, ordinary people—store clerks, laborers, students at business schools or at the secondary school; one was a bank clerk. They were not like the revolutionaries I had known, but much humbler and cruder. It was doubtlessly a heterogeneous mass gathered by Fidel from among the various elements of the Cuban people he came in contact with. Their language was coarse, and from the things they said I thought some of them irresponsible. Fidel, calm, noble of bearing, stood out among them like a tower among hovels. Later I came to understand that this was the basis of his absolute authority over them; it was why he was able to impose an extremely rigid discipline upon them, from which he and his three or four closest associates were exempt. But then, thinking these things, I reminded myself that the commonness of those men was overlaid by the quality of their purpose; and if they were rough and uneducated, it was because they had never been given the opportunity to be otherwise.

In the prison yard a bell was rung; visiting time was over. Fidel immediately returned to me. As we took leave of each other, I gave him my card and said that if I could ever be of aid he was to consider my house his own. This is a common expression of cordiality among Spanish-speaking peoples. How literally he was to take it, you will soon see.

Before we left they all came together and sang the Cuban national anthem—out of tune and inharmoniously. In all frankness, I was ashamed of my embarrassment at this demonstration of patriotic ardor, which seemed to me to be a bit old-fashioned and ridiculous—what you Americans call "corny."

As Lilia and I left that big grass yard with its old fountain in the middle I had no idea that my life was already set on a new course, and that as a consequence of this visit I was to return four months later, this time as a prisoner.

chapter

6

Before meeting Fidel Castro in the Immigration Prison I knew nothing at all about him, but thinking about him afterwards, I thought I remembered having heard his name mentioned in connection with an attempt in 1953 to storm and capture the Moncada barracks in Santiago de Cuba. Information had been scanty about that attack, and the only thing I had been able to learn was that it had met with dismal failure. It was only later that I was able to piece together enough facts to trace his movements and development from his student days at the university to the time of his imprisonment in Mexico.

As a student he was to some extent affiliated with the hoodlum gangs that were prevalent at the university during the Grau administration. Those gangs involved themselves in the country's politics, and it was probably this point that interested Fidel. It is unlikely that he participated in their armed attacks.

In 1948 he attended a student congress in Bogotá, Colombia, as a member of the Cuban delegation. While he was there a revolt took place in the city, in which priests and nuns were killed. As far as I know, there is no truth to the story that Fidel had a hand in those killings. In Mexico, once, when someone mentioned "the Bogotá business," he laughed and gestured at Rafael del Pino, saying, "He's the one who got me into the whole mess, because he had the idea that we should go from the hotel to the Cuban embassy during all the shooting." Fidel was twenty-two at the time, and given his temperament, it is easy to imagine him mixing with that violent mob that went running through the streets of Bogotá. But those statistics of priests and nuns supposedly killed by him in the middle of the tumult and confusion appeared only after his emergence as an internationally known figure. And they are the harder to believe in light of the fact that the Church, which as a social organism can hardly be said to be ill informed, always helped him afterwards. The archbishop of Santiago de Cuba saved his life after the Moncada attack, and the Church later gave him its support during the two years that he spent in the Sierra Maestra in the revolution that deposed Batista.

Another incident that took place in his student days was an abortive expedition to the Dominican Republic. About a thousand expeditionaries were preparing to sail from Cayo Confite, in northern Oriente Province, with the purpose of overthrowing Trujillo, when President Grau's Chief of Staff had them disarmed and removed to Havana. To escape capture, Fidel swam the enormous shark-infested Bay of Nipe, which is the largest in Cuba.

In 1952, shortly after his graduation with a law doctorate, he was campaigning for a congressional post in the approaching elections to determine Prío's successor when Batista frustrated him with the coup of March 10. As a lawyer, Fidel Castro then presented a petition in the Supreme Court demanding that the Batista government be declared unconstitutional and therefore illegal. Thereafter he was to call repeatedly for the reinstallation of the Constitution of 1940. Prío's party, incidentally, was losing ground with the electorate at the time of the coup, and had little chance of winning the elections had they been held. One of the chief reasons for Prío's decline of popularity was the bitter and unrelenting public denunciations by Eduardo Chibás, who is important in any review of the personal development of Fidel Castro because it was Chibás who was his model and political mentor. Chibás, angry because Prío had been picked as his party's presidential candidate over himself, had formed a splinter party and dedicated himself to attacking the Prío government with a series of long, incendiary speeches. It is probably from him that Fidel got his proclivity for endless, fulminating perorations. Chibás was a hysterical man who had once turned imminent defeat into victory, in a constituents election, by returning from a lone automobile ride to the outskirts of Havana with a bullet wound and a story about having been attacked in the dark by political assassins. The resulting outcry brought him victory on that occasion, but he was less fortunate in 1952. Shortly before Batista's coup, at the height of despair because he could not furnish the documentary proof against Prío's Minister of Education that he had promised, he shot himself in front of the television cameras, and died two or three days later. His impassioned oratory had inspired a kind of devotion and even adoration in the people, and I think Fidel always dreamed of capturing that irrational mass reverence for himself.

On July 26, 1953, Fidel led a small band of men armed with a few old rifles and pistols in an assault on the Moncada post in Santiago de Cuba. Their plan was to capture the armory, take the post, win over the soldiers, and arouse the Cuban people against Batista. The plan had no provision for failure or retreat. When they shot their way past the surprised sentries and found the armory empty of arms—owing to a coming social event for which it was to be used—they retreated in total disorder. It was a massacre, and with few exceptions, those who were not killed were captured. One of those exceptions was Fidel. He fled into the nearby mountains, and just as he was about to be caught—probably tortured and shot —the archbishop of Santiago de Cuba, wishing to stop further bloodshed, arranged for his safe surrender. He was put in the Santiago prison, where, before he was tried, orders were given to a Captain Jesús Yanes Pelletier to poison him. Captain Yanes not only refused to do it but spread word through the city about what he had been told to do, and thus prevented the order from being carried out by someone else. For this the captain was courtmartialed, imprisoned, and expelled from the army. He eventually went into exile in the United States and joined the revolutionary movement. Fidel was tried and sent to the Isle of Pines for fifteen years, along with his brother, Raúl Castro, and a few other survivors of the Moncada assault. It was at this trial that Fidel made his famous "History Will Absolve Me" speech.

When it was discovered that Fidel was smuggling out messages and articles for publication, he was put in solitary confinement. Before elections in 1955, and two years after Fidel's arrest, a general amnesty for political prisoners was given. Fidel went to Mexico, and then to the United States, where he founded the Movement of the Twenty-sixth of July (M26-7) in honor of the Moncada attack. With the movement established in Tampa, New York, and one or two other cities, he returned to Mexico, where he met Che Guevara, who had fled there after the fall of the Leftist government in Guatemala. At that time the movement was small, but soon volunteers and money began to arrive from its supporters in the United States and Cuba. Paying their own way whenever possible, the future expeditionaries went into training on a ranch Fidel had rented not far from Mexico City. They were trained, at the beginning, by a former captain in the Spanish Republican Army, Alberto Bayo, whom they called, good-naturedly, "Colonel." Bayo was a pleasant, harmless man in his sixties; he played a much smaller part in the movement than is generally believed, and was not a Communist, as has been stated by those who maintain that the movement was riddled with Communists from its very inception. (I met only one Marxist, besides Guevara, among the expeditionaries, and he was the constant butt of his companions' jokes.) Soon after Fidel's spoken and written promise that the expeditionaries would land on Cuba before the end of 1956, the Mexican police raided the ranch and sent the expeditionaries to the Immigration Prison.

From all this it is apparent that Fidel Castro has lived a "charmed" life, for he has escaped the most incredible dangers without a scratch. Obviously, too, he is a courageous man, and a born warrior. It also becomes apparent, however, that the danger in many cases was heightened by recklessness and a lack of rational appraisal and preparation, which, if they spared him, did not spare many of his devoted companions, and which, had I not been totally ignorant of the man's past life when I met him, might have given me pause in our subsequent interview.

chapter

7

Two days after my visit to the Immigration Prison, at about five o'clock in the afternoon, I opened the door of my house to find Fidel Castro seated on the sofa at the far end of the drawing room, shaking his head in mock reproach. He had been waiting for over an hour. We got down to the business at hand almost at once, and he did not leave until eleven o'clock that night.

The business at hand was the revolution. For revolutions, enthusiasm is essential, and this I did not have. I had extended an invitation, which he had accepted. Now I stood at the crossroads. But I could not easily surrender to his ardor and confidence—I had seen too much of that. I would not lightly accept a "messiah," a "savior of Cuba." I had known many people of high quality to compare him with, and enough of low quality to be on my guard. And I was in a discouraged frame of mind. Knowing my people's mood, and the spirit of irresponsibility to which it had abandoned itself, I was unable to believe in it once more and to hope for a resurgence of heroism at the signal of another would-be liberator.

But Fidel had a young man's exuberant faith in the Cuban people. At the moment of truth we would not be alone, he said. The people would rise up and help him to overthrow the dictator.

But that was just it: would they do this?

I gazed implacably at Fidel's face, observing his speech,

his vocabulary, his manner of expressing himself, interrupting constantly although I was eager to be convinced by him. I reminded him of the solitude and silence that had accompanied his attempt to take the Moncada barracks in 1953, and I asked him for proof that Cuba was, as he claimed, helping his revolutionary movement.

He replied that in every village on the island collections were being made, and the pennies, nickels, and dimes the poor folk contributed were sent to him for the sustenance, training, and equipping of the volunteers who for several months had been coming from Cuba to join his band of liberators. He had little to say about the Moncada incident, or about himself. He did not make himself out to be a messiah or an aspirant savior of Cuba. His basic point, the fixed star of his faith, was the people: the people wanted to be liberated, and backed his movement because he was trying to overthrow Batista, and he would do it. He had a serene firmness that was more convincing than if he had raised his voice in flaming grandiloquence, in the style of other would-be popular leaders.

Fidel Castro asked for nothing that day. He only wanted me to talk of various figures of the Generation of the Thirties who seemed especially to interest him. He listened, absorbing whatever he considered to be a contribution to his knowledge. He struck me as being a man who would never underestimate the value of anyone; everybody was important to him. And what of his band of liberators? I expressed my sincere belief that the young men I had met in the jail appeared to me to be well intentioned but incapable of being the directors of a movement of national reorganization. He assured me that such was not their function; that in Cuba the twenty-sixth of July movement, had the active participation of brave and capable intellectuals who were already co-operating in the organization and reconstruction of the future Cuba; that his group of young men were there solely for the purpose of liberating the country as soldiers disposed to sacrifice themselves, and were not concerned with reconstruction.

My feeling was that if by some miracle—I saw it that way; and his arrival on Cuban shores was in fact nothing else *but* a miracle—Fidel and those naïve souls he led ever managed to set foot on our soil, neither he nor they stood much of a chance of living to tell about it. I tried to convince him to find some other formula for liberating Cuba. But it was I who was convinced by him that in dealing with Batista and his army there was no other way but to wage "the necessary war," as Martí had called the one waged for our independence. Fidel showed that he had read a great deal of José Martí, who seemed, indeed, to be the guiding spirit of his life. That Fidel was by his nature a man of war, and Martí a man of peace, was a fundamental contradiction which time has brought into sharp relief, and which I had no way of recognizing at the time.

The plans he revealed seemed beyond his reach, and I felt a kind of pity for this aspiring deliverer who was so full of confidence and firm conviction. I was moved by his innocence. I had known so many like him whose dreams had been shattered by life's realities. But during that long conversation I began to have a feeling of esteem for him and sympathy for his cause. My past appeared to join with his present and with Cuba's future. True, I could not give myself up to the intense admiration which he inspired in his group of young men, and I thought from the start that there was something of the irresponsible, irrepressible child in him, of a child taking on tasks for which he was lacking in both preparation and capacity; but I was immediately fond of him, and I respected him; and Martí's writings could guide him. It was not for me, I thought, to establish prerequisites for superiority in any man. Even before he left, I had already more or less decided to help him all I could, because, after all, whether or not he suited the role, his revolution was of and for the Cuban people.

I think he stretched our conversation a little, hoping that Lilia, who had dined out with friends, would arrive before he left. When he was gone, I sat contemplating this new turn my life was taking. I did not trouble myself to weigh the pros and cons. I had already done that during our talk. I was in need of a dream, and this young man had one, a worthy one, in which I could share. I needed to have faith in something once again. My past life had come to seem meaningless. I had begun to think that my people did not deserve the sacrifice of so many noble patriots as I had seen killed or broken in its name, and who now seemed condemned to oblivion. Now I could have my faith back. Now, too, I could come down spiritedly from my cultivated and lonely ivory tower and place myself cheerfully, hopefully among the rest of humanity.

But there was another reason lurking in my soul, and it may have been the most profoundly influential motive of all. Fidel and his band of young men seemed to me to be a lost cause. And—perhaps it is a residue of those defeats of my adolescent days—I have always been a lover of lost causes.

The next evening Fidel was back. Cándido González, tall, swarthy, handsome, lithe, very strong, and very quiet, was with him. Cándido was his right-hand man, one of his two "guardian angels," as Lilia baptized them, and his inseparable companion. He was the spirit of silent, uncomplaining self-sacrifice. I had not seen him on my visit to the jail because he was one of those who had been tortured by the police. He had borne three days of torture without uttering a word of information.

Fidel had come to ask me if I could keep "a few things" for him. He thought the Mexican police were getting ready to close in on his hide-outs, and it was urgently necessary to get those things to a place of safety. He did not say what those things were. Naturally my answer was yes; but I showed him a cable I had received from a Cuban girl who was arriving in Mexico that same night expecting to stay with me. I took him upstairs to show him the only one of my closets fitted with a lock, so that he might judge whether it would hold his "few things," and his optimistic reply was: "Easily. But you must get rid of that girl. She can't come here." In such a way, with his charmingly urgent, preoccupied air, did he take possession of my house. But my lot was cast with the revolutionaries, and the tradition of hospitality was only the first, and smallest, of the sacrifices I was expected to make. From then on, the house would have to be free for the comings and goings of the liberators.

Fortunately another cable arrived: my friend's trip had met with a slight delay. It gave me time to write her an absurd letter excusing myself for not being able to put her up in my house. I found her a reasonably priced room in a Cuban woman's home, and saw her so rarely during her sojourn in Mexico—inviting her to visit me only once—that the poor girl returned to Cuba with the idea that I was a fickle friend, and sadly lacking in hospitality. From that first night onward, indeed, I was a monster of bad manners, driving away my friends who planned on visiting me. Much time had to pass, and a renowned event to take place, before they would be able to understand, retrospectively, the reason for my unsociable behavior.

That night Fidel and his men returned with the "few things" I was to keep for them, which turned out to be a veritable arsenal, seven carloads of munitions. They filled my house with terrible and frightening instruments of death that kept me distracted and sleepless for days. There were machine guns, bayonets, pistols, rifles with telescopic sights, and long and sinister bullets that were very different from what I had used in my little 22-gauge shotgun as a girl. Moreover, I had never used them to shoot at a living thing. The operation had to be carried out in the dead of night while the servants slept in their separate bungalow. Lilia played the hi-fi set very loud, so that the neighbors would think I was having a fiesta. Most of the men left with the automobiles as soon as they were unloaded. Then Fidel remained below conversing with Lilia, with the music lowered to a more reasonable volume, while Cándido and I set about accommodating part of the arsenal in Lilia's room. Rafael del Pino, Fidel's other "guardian angel," did the same with my closet, after I had emptied it out. While helping Cándido unpack, I noticed what looked like a peculiar weapon. When I asked him what "that knife there" was, and he replied that it was not a knife but part of a bayonet, I felt a pain in my stomach as if my solar plexus were being run through.

I had to make myself understand. In order to fight against a well-equipped army it was necessary to use arms. We of the former revolution had failed in our general strike of March 1935 because there had been no armed movement to back it up. I thought of Machado's famous reply to the student manifestos of 1930: "I am not going to be overthrown by scraps of paper." The "scraps of paper," alone, had failed against Machado in 1930 and against Batista in 1935. Cuban youth had learned that lesson.

Of course the arms did not fit into the one closet. Others had to be requisitioned and their doors nailed up to avoid their being opened thoughtlessly by an unsuspecting maid. I had to put all my clothes into one closet, and some nights later I was awakened by a muffled crash that sounded as if a closet floor had given way; but it was only the bar in my new clothes closet that had broken under the weight of all the jammed-in coats and dresses.

When Cándido and I had finished storing thirty thousand bullets in metal boxes—"one face-up, the next face-down"—we went downstairs to the drawing room, where Fidel had been talking with Lilia all that time. She was dying for sleep and went up to bed. Rafael del Pino was sound asleep on my bed. For the rest of us, the night's work was just beginning.

Cándido, who had carried almost all the equipment upstairs by himself, with that incredible agile strength in his wiry arms, was exhausted. But now Fidel had him fetch my typewriter, and, lighting fresh cigars, they settled down in the dining room to do a long article for a Cuban magazine, Fidel dictating and pacing the floor while Cándido typed. The article was to be carried to Cuba by someone who was leaving for the island that noon. When it was almost finished, Cándido went for their rented automobile, which stood, prudently, two blocks away, and I replaced him at the typewriter. The article was to appear under the name of some other member of the band, and it closed with a series of eulogies in capital letters, in praise of the group's "highest chief," the "great leader," Fidel Castro. I stopped and advised him not to use the capital letters. I pointed out how shocking an impression it made. For a moment he seemed annoyed. Then, recovering his usual manner, he explained that it was important to inspire faith in the people towards one person. He said he too disliked such things, but they were necessary. . . .

With the exception of the "Pact of Mexico"—a compromise between the new Cuban "Revolutionary Directorate" of students and the M26–7—which we did a month later, he never again dictated to me or made me privy to his official documents. (To fulfill the Pact, more than fifty lives were sacrificed when the Directorate students bravely assaulted the Presidential Palace on March 13, 1957.)

From that day on, Fidel and his men would come calling at the most unexpected hours. They would clean their rifles in my room while I, if it was daytime, stood watch to make sure the servants did not wander in. Or they would wrap the rifles in a quilt and carry them off to their training ranch near the U.S. border—a three-day journey by automobile and horse. There, amid cactus, woods, and poisonous snakes, the future expeditionaries toughened and trained themselves, and were instructed in guerrilla warfare by "Colonel" Bayo.

When the house adjacent to mine became vacant, Fidel asked me to take it on a lease for some volunteers he was expecting from Cuba. The house had furniture and was owned by the same woman who owned mine. One of those volunteers was an old comrade of Fidel's who knew more about the handling, care, and repair of weapons than anyone else in the band. He was Pedro Miret, who was later to be Fidel's Minister of Agriculture.

Pedro was a last-year student of engineering at the University of Havana when he participated in that unsuccessful attempt to take the Moncada barracks. When Fidel and his sorely pressed rebels withdrew, Pedro covered their retreat until a bullet creased his forehead. Being taken for dead, he was thrown into a yard among a mass of dead companions. Most of the corpses were horribly mutilated by castration, blinding, etc., and the grim pile was added to while he lay unconscious, so that he was almost buried under them. When he regained his senses, bathed in blood, and understood what had happened, he lay still until things had quieted down, then called to an officer passing by who seemed to him to have the face of a decent man. At first the officer was terrified to hear a dead man calling to him from that pile of corpses, but he saved Pedro's life by carrying him to the hospital. There, sadistic soldier-nurses experimented with him, trying to inject air into his veins to see if he would die. In spite of everything Pedro lived, and was finally tried and sentenced to the Isle of Pines Penitentiary for fifteen years. On his release from prison in the general amnesty he went into hiding, then fled to Mexico. We had three other survivors of the ill-starred battle. Pedro used to say that anyone who had survived that action was immortal.

I took the house for six months in the fictional name of some compatriot friends who would be coming to spend a season in Mexico. As Pedro was bringing his wife, there would be little to attract attention. When they arrived, it was agreed that there must be no communication between us, not even polite greetings, so as to avoid drawing the attention of the neighbors. They became, in fact, the most silent and unsociable Cubans imaginable. There was one exception—Miguelito, a young worker in the Cuban cigar industry, who would slip away in an afternoon to have coffee with me and keep me company in my lonely vigil. I had to stay at home in case the men came for their weapons or had need of something. Like the others, Miguelito would show me pictures of his wife and little daughter. Through such photographs I came to know many wives, mothers, sisters, and fiancées whom I afterwards met when official mourning for those dead youths brought us together after the victory.

The house next door became another arms depot. Pedro Miret gave the apprentice expeditionaries pointers about shooting and the handling of arms, just as he had done for the Moncada assault. When the weapons came back from the ranch for cleaning and repair, he would bend over them, with that great scar on his forehead, and examine and care for them with his expert hands. The weapons were always dirty and even rusty, and Pedro constantly reproached Fidel for their condition and for allowing such slovenliness to continue.

As the days and weeks went by, the romance between Lilia and Fidel flowered. He sought her out with a youthful effusiveness and impetuosity that both startled and amused her. The amusement gave her an appearance of imperturbability which, combined with her great beauty, enchanted him, although it may also have been the quality which finally exasperated him, for Fidel cannot suffer people to remain unconquerable before him. We often went to some out-of-the-way place to eat, Fidel, Lilia, the quiet Cándido, and I. There was a picturesque restaurant on top of a hill outside the city that Fidel especially favored. Cándido and I liked each other's company enough to have enjoyed being left alone together if Fidel and Lilia had gone off by themselves. But, although I did not know it at the time, Cándido had been expressly ordered by Fidel to have no relationship with me other than that connected with the revolution. This explained Cándido's sudden reticence in my regard, and his peculiar behavior on the few occasions that he came to my house unaccompanied. Once he squeezed me with impulsive strength between his arms, without a word, then abruptly left the house, leaving the weapon he had been cleaning lying on the floor of my room. Another time, when he had come into my room to get some guns, he asked me to stay in the farthest corner until he left, and not to look at him. I was mystified, but he never offered me an explanation, and it was only after his death that I learned from Lilia and her mother that he had been following Fidel's orders. It is possible that Fidel, who was well aware of Cándido's strong attraction for women, wished as my friend to spare me a problem of that kind. However, it may also have irritated him that wherever they went together, feminine interest was directed at Cándido and not at himself. Lilia had once mentioned Cándido's good looks to Fidel, and after that Cándido was rarely invited along on their outings.

Whatever the reason, my house was by Fidel's orders out of bounds for almost all of his men, with the exception of Cándido, and one or two others who never came alone. I never again saw Che Guevara in Mexico, nor did I meet Raúl Castro, though both were in Mexico all that time. And despite our rapport and mutual attraction—or because of them—Cándido and I were forced by his puzzling reticence on the one hand, and my affronted, baffled pride on the other, into a strained silence whose memory aches me to this day, but which I gather met with the paternal approval of our young Alexander. On August 13, for his thirtieth birthday, I gave Fidel a gift. It was, ironically, a German straight razor I knew he admired and which, as the world knows, he would soon have little use for. With visible emotion, he said that it was the only present he had received, that he would never forget it and would keep it for the rest of his life. How I wish I could have offered Cándido some token of my affection for him! But shortly before his own thirtieth birthday he was dead, along with more than half of Fidel's expeditionary force.

Fidel, remember, had announced to the world at large, and in writing, that he and his men would land on Cuban soil before the year 1956 went out. In order to keep this promise, which he considered a vital necessity if he was to inspire confidence in the Cuban people, he began to rush his preparations for the expedition. Most of all he needed money. Because Carlos Prío, the ex-President of Cuba, was a dear friend of mine and a wealthy man, Fidel wanted to meet him. He asked me to go to Prío in Miami and arrange an interview, cautioning me, however, to let Prío be the one to suggest the meeting.

I was in Miami five days. The negotiations were successful: Carlos was eager to talk to Fidel, and a rendezvous was arranged. They were to meet a week later at a specified place in the United States, just over the border. Prío suggested a certain "connection"—an important Mexican political figure—for getting Fidel across the border, but Fidel, who had been given two weeks to get out of Mexico on his release from prison and was now in the country illegally, preferred not to take the risk, and swam the Río Grande instead. When he returned, he told me I was right to praise Prío's humanity and nobility of character. But Fidel, who must always be first in everything, was infuriated when I described Carlos as my best friend, and one who had never let me down.

"And I? What am I—the second best?" he said.

As a result of their meeting, Prío helped to sustain the expense of two years of costly expeditions—many of which fell into the hands of U.S. authorities—and clandestine shipments of arms and men. The yacht *Gramma* in which Fidel and his eighty-one expeditionaries sailed from Mexico was bought with money received from him.

When I got back from Miami I found that Fidel had made a proposal of marriage to Lilia, and she had accepted. She had left her job at the music store and was living at home with her parents while they rested between cultural lecture tours. Very formally and correctly Fidel had obtained their consent. As part of her trousseau, he had equipped her with new clothes, shoes, a large bottle of French perfume, and a pretty bathing suit to replace her French bikini, which infuriated him. I have no idea where he got the money for all this; according to Lilia, he received only eighty dollars each month from his family. Yet he spent money freely, even alarmingly. Some of it was generosity, as when he offered to pay my rent after learning of my financial troubles from Lilia—an offer I refused; and some of it was sheer necessity, as in the bribes he was forced to give the Mexican police to overlook the fact of his illegal presence in the country, and not to interfere with his secret movements and arms purchases. Batista continually sent gifts to the Mexican authorities, and Fidel had to follow suit in self-defense.

Fidel's plan was to marry Lilia and take her with him on the expedition. (He also invited me along.) But their engagement lasted less than a month. Lilia's parents went away on another lecture tour and she came back to live with me. Each day found Fidel busier than the day before, trying frantically to get the expedition off the ground. He knew that another expedition was being made ready in the Dominican Republic, and it was his obsession to be first "so as not to be confused with those others." (That expedition, which never materialized, was also financed by Prío.) In any case, he had made that promise to land in Cuba before the end of the year, and it was now September. He hardly ever had time to see Lilia, and when he did drop by, it was never for more than a few minutes. Now that she had had time to think about it, she saw that their natures were opposed; her gentleness was incompatible with Fidel's overriding fieriness. She was not happy at the prospect of being carried off on an expeditionary adventure and to a war. The very act of getting married posed a problem, for, as Fidel was an illegal resident, it would be necessary to go to some small village in the interior and bribe a judge to perform the ceremony. For another thing, Lilia had become inflated with vanity and was all but unbearable. Fidel had taken her to the homes of his followers, who had flattered her outrageously, calling her "the future First Lady of Cuba," and so forth. I think even Fidel was somewhat put off by her sudden air of importance. The whole thing came to a head when Lilia's ex-fiancé returned to Mexico, assured her that he could not live without her, and offered to marry her immediately, with the simple wedding she had wanted.

She told Fidel about it that same night. Considering it an ultimatum, Fidel, with that terrible pride of his, told her to marry the other man, that he was "better suited" to her.

The next morning I heard steps in Lilia's room. It was quite early; normally she slept very late, now that she was not working, and had breakfast in bed. I found her dressed for a trip, with her suitcase already packed. She said that she was very sorry to leave Fidel in this abrupt manner but that she and her young Mexican were off to rejoin her parents and be married. She gave me the job of telling Fidel of her decision.

It was an unpleasant assignment. When he arrived to call for her and I had to tell him she was gone, I knew that thereafter he might associate me with a bad experience. But he took the news with marvelous serenity. He made me touch his hands to see that they were neither cold nor trembling. He said he had already understood that Lilia was not for him, and that it would be better this way. At that moment the telephone rang. Lilia was calling from the airport: the take-off was slightly delayed. Fidel asked me to give him the receiver and, with admirably friendly calm, reminded Lilia that he himself had advised her to do what she was going to do. He said he felt no rancor but asked one favor of her: that she never speak of the secrets she knew, nor of the houses she had visited with him.

On the following day she was married. They never saw each other again. Fidel reverted to his pre-Lilia habits and stopped bathing and dressing neatly and enjoying the things natural to those of his age—gaiety, music, excursions. Instead, he spent his free time in the upper rooms with his equipment, examining and re-examining it for hours. He liked to raise his favorite rifle—which was of Belgian make and, he said, a beautiful weapon—and aim it between the shutters at the television antenna of the house opposite. They were all like that, fondling those weapons like happy kids. One day the Chief of Immigration of Mexico sent a message: "Tell Fidel Castro and his boys to stop playing cowboys and Indians; they are too big for that."

One night not long after Lilia's marriage I went into her room. On the bed lay the parts of a machine gun, and some pistols, and beside them lay Fidel with his legs doubled up, rocking contentedly like a little boy with his favorite toy.

"Now I do have a beautiful fiancée!" he said happily.

"Another one?"

"Yes—the revolution!"

And so it was. Since Lilia, no woman has been able to interest him seriously, although hundreds have tried. He has no other fiancée than "his" revolution.

After Lilia left, Cándido thought it would be wise to move all the armament out of the two houses, in case of an indiscretion on her part. Fidel decided it was not necessary, and he was right: she never said a word. Betrayal, when it came, wore the features of Rafael del Pino, one of the "guardian angels."

I began to see very little of Fidel and Cándido. With Lilia gone and with only a few months left before Fidel's self-imposed invasion deadline, their visits were few and very brief. I tried very hard to get Fidel to attend at least one of the sessions at the Congress for Cultural Freedom then being held in Mexico, but he was always "very busy." Only two members of the Cuban delegation interested him: Mario Llerena, a revolutionary collaborator whom he already knew, and Raúl Roa, whom he wished to meet. But Raúl was not interested in meeting Fidel. Because of Fidel's association with the student gangs while still at the university, Raúl's impression was of a young political hoodlum who would not pursue the revolution's true goals. Fidel sat in my house for most of one night waiting to go to Roa's hotel on the eve of Raúl's departure, while I kept calling Raúl, only to be put off with excuses again and again.

When, in November, they began to take things out of the closets, and did not bring them back, I realized that the day of their departure was approaching, although nothing precise was said to me. Each time they came they said, "Today makes it so-and-so-many days until the end of the year. We won't be here much longer." But the only thing that indicated actual preparations was their taking those few things from the closets. I had pointed out to Fidel that he ought to obtain his provisions for the expedition ahead of time, and had offered to take care of that operation for him. He had said yes, but time passed and he said nothing more about it. Evidently he did not want me to know until the last minute when they would be leaving, although it is also likely that he himself did not know; they had not yet purchased the vessel that was to carry them to Cuban shores. The first idea had been to buy an old Catalina Flying Boat in the United States, and the decision to go by sea was made only after negotiations for the air transport fell through. This and other misadventures, it would appear, called for a delay in the scheduled departure of the expedition, particularly when Melba Hernández de Montané, who was one of the two female survivors of the Moncada assault, returned from a trip to Cuba with the report that our country had absolutely no preparations under way for helping Fidel's invasion, and that an expedition at that moment was inadvisable. Though subsequent events bore out the accuracy of her report, she was accused of "defeatism" in a stormy session that lasted a whole night.

Obviously no practical considerations were going to prevent Fidel from trying to get to Cuba before the end of 1956, and when Rafael del Pino understood this fact, the "guardian angel" shed his wings. He was enjoying life in Mexico, living moderately well and avoiding training for an expedition he thought would never actually materialize. Perhaps because he was older than the others and had some experience of shooting revolutions, he had little enthusiasm for what he knew would be a very dangerous adventure, whose outcome was extremely doubtful. He began inventing pretexts and feigning illness, and finally

116

he ran away from the training ranch. Two weeks after his desertion, the police came to my house with a detailed list of the supplies to be found there. Rafael had gone all the way, and turned into Lucifer.

In the adjacent house they arrested **Pedro Miret** and **Ennio Leyva**—a very young man who had been sent back from the ranch because he had not yet recovered from a vicious beating he had received from the police in Havana. Even a most spirited protest by my loyal Tere was to no avail, and I was taken with the two men to the Immigration Prison, where we were put in separate dark rooms. We were questioned all night long with the object of making us acknowledge that it was Fidel who was behind the arms cache.

The story I made up was that some Cubans, whose names I did not know, had left those boxes in my keeping; when they failed to return, I opened them and, seeing what they contained and realizing that they were intended to be used against Batista, decided to hide them. Such broad hospitality was not entirely incredible, for the police had seen that my garage was full of boxes and empty suitcases that I was keeping for a theatrical group, and for a friend of mine, respectively. They took turns questioning me, but I stuck to my story. I later had the satisfaction of learning that Fidel was fully informed, by a policeman friend of his, of my comportment in the "grillings."

We were held incommunicado for eight days. The only thing permitted us was the food my faithful Tere brought for us daily. (In those days there was no cook in the Immigration Prison; in any case the food in Mexican jails was frightful.) On the eighth day, a Sunday, we were allowed a visitor—Lilia's mother. She told me that the boys were all right but had disappeared from circulation to elude the police. Every evening, she said, Cándido called

117

her and asked the same question: "How is Teté?" She would say I was all right, and he would hang up.

The night before—Saturday—he had called as usual. It was the last time he called, and I have since learned that it was the last thing he did before leaving Mexico City forever. For at one o'clock on that same Sunday morning of November 25, 1956, Fidel Castro and eighty-one companions had set sail for Cuba aboard the yacht *Gramma*. Even while I stood talking to Lilia's mother in the same prison courtyard where I had first met them, the expeditionaries were already at sea, twelve hours from the Mexican shore.

chapter

8

From the Immigration Prison I was sent to the Federal Prison for five days, then to a dark, cold dungeon in a jail that dated back to the Inquisition. There I was held for fifteen hours while waiting to be indicted. It was five degrees below freezing, and I and the six women delinquents with whom I shared the dungeon tried to keep warm by swinging our arms and even running from wall to wall. There was a small window high up which let a few rays of light into the cell, and through it a folded-up newspaper suddenly flew in and fell to the stone floor. I opened it and read the headline:

REVOLUTION BREAKS OUT IN CUBA

The other women helped me up to the window. It looked out on a big central yard, where Melba Hernández de Montané stood smiling up at me, her eyes bright with tears. I could hardly speak, and held up the newspaper questioningly.

"Yes," she said, her voice breaking with emotion, "they left last Sunday."

"And your husband?"

"He is with them. They are in Cuba. *They are fighting.*"

My companions helped me down. I read the account. It said only that a revolt had broken out in Santiago de Cuba. There was no mention of Castro or the expedition.

But they were there. The leader of the underground in Santiago de Cuba, Frank País, had come to Mexico over a month ago to synchronize the revolt in Santiago with the landing of the expeditionaries. If the revolt had broken out, it meant that the expeditionaries had landed. And I was in jail, and there was nothing I could do except try not to go out of my mind with anxiety and frustration, and struggle against my claustrophobia.

The three of us, Pedro, Ennio, and I, were indicted for "accumulating arms." Bail was first set at a quarter of a million pesos each. The Cuban embassy was exerting strong pressure on the authorities to prevent our release, and particularly that of Pedro Miret. They thought Fidel could not possibly have left for Cuba after the loss of his military supplies and the arrest of his arms expert, and that he was still in Mexico. Keeping Pedro in jail, they thought, was one way to keep Fidel in Mexico. When it was known that he was in Cuba, our bail was lowered to thirty thousand pesos ($2,400) each—quite a drop, but still thirty times the customary amount for the offense.

Of course we were unable to raise bail—the bond companies demanded a counter-signer, in the bargain, and who would risk his property as guarantee for a foreigner who was probably secretly planning to return to his own country?—and we were put back in jail. I was sent to the Woman's Prison, sixteen miles from Mexico City. Once a week my faithful cook was permitted to visit me. She would come loaded down with packages of food and cigarettes, and cry with indignation at my plight. I escaped the mandatory month of forced labor in the fields through the kindly intervention of another prisoner, who had me certified as medically unfit for forced labor, and I was assigned to the sewing room instead. This prisoner was one of two who took a protective interest in me and saved me from the humiliations and even blows to which all newcomers were normally subjected at the hands of a clique of hardened inmates. They made life a little more bearable in a prison where the chief luxury was an ice-cold shower at five o'clock in the morning, if the water was not frozen.

The guard in the sewing room had a small son who was permitted to enter the workrooms, and he would smuggle newspapers in for the prisoners, who liked to read the criminal reports. A few days after my admittance, the boy came over to me, handed me a newspaper, and whispered, "Fidel Castro and all his friends have been killed." I sank onto a bench clutching the newspaper and stared at the bulletin. The expeditionaries had been wiped out as soon as they had landed. An American correspondent for the United Press named Francis L. McCarthy reported that the corpses of Fidel and Raúl Castro, and of all the others, were in Manzanillo. His details were convincing.

For the rest of that morning I was literally blind. The words of the dispatch danced before my eyes. The prisoners talked, sewed, chattered about their lawyers, their hopes of leaving soon, boasted of their crimes. It was like a whirlpool of sound. The guard who was the boy's mother came up to me, looking frightened, and begged me not to cry or show that I had read a newspaper, or she would suffer for it. I stared numbly at her. Cry? I could not have cried even if it had occurred to me.

At that moment I was told to report to the prison office, where I was to be fingerprinted, photographed with a number on my chest, and classified for the seventh time in a few days. I went alone, slipping away from my two constant companions. I felt a desperate need to be absolutely alone, if only for a few minutes. The dining hall was practically empty and I sat down in a little patch of sunlight that entered through one of the high windows. It was the first sun I had seen in that jail. When I looked up, it was to see myself surrounded by a gang of inmates who looked more like men than like women. It was the tough clique, smarting at not having been able to give me the usual treatment accorded to new prisoners. Their chief held out a dirty rag and said, "Go over there and scrub the floor where you threw the food."

I had not touched food. It took me a moment to understand that she was talking to me. What she was saying was that I had a choice between being humiliated and being beaten. I focused on those morbid faces twisted with malicious laughter. This was exactly what I needed —something to fight against, something to hurl my rage and pain and impotence against. I would have liked to fight, to scream, to tear down the walls if it were possible. I don't know what they saw in my eyes, but they stood dumfounded. Very deliberately I said, "Do you know why I am here? For keeping an arsenal of guns and bullets in my house. I am sure you have seen it in the newspapers."

I got up slowly and stood as if ready to charge. "Get out of my way." The women moved aside, I walked away— slowly, for I was still in a mood to fight, even if I should be torn to pieces.

The other prisoners were delighted. They had suffered the insults and humiliations of that maffia with humble patience. Now they could retaliate with jokes and jibes. They became very friendly toward me and, as a sign of special favor, arranged for me to have a tepid bath in the room of one of the guards.

For over three weeks I was in one jail or another—five in all. I suffer terribly from claustrophobia, and in all of them I had to use all my strength to dominate the sensation that I was suffocating and that I had been buried alive, especially in my lone cell in the Mexico City Penitentiary with its solid iron door bolted on the outside, and I incommunicado within, perspiring continuously despite the sub-zero temperatures. At first I tried to think of the others, fighting for their lives in Cuba; but after the bulletin reporting their deaths, I had to try *not* to think of them, or of Cuba, or of my life, or of anything, for every thought then was treacherous, a pang of despair.

Twenty-four days after our arrest we were able to get out on bail. The money, once again, came from my never-failing friend in Miami, Carlos Prío. I went home, alone, and let myself into my house, my empty house. The boys' ghosts were everywhere.

chapter

9

Little by little the news reports showed the inaccuracy of Francis L. McCarthy's information. It was not known whether Fidel Castro was alive or dead. The landing had gone very badly, and a great many expeditionaries had been killed, but not all. The rest had moved on, their destination the Sierra Maestra. Neither Fidel nor Raúl had been killed on the first day as McCarthy had reported.

Then, just before Christmas, I read a newspaper interview of a survivor of the early fighting who had been captured. In it I learned of the death of Cándido and of many others for whom I had come to feel a fondness, among them young Miguelito, who had so often shown me photographs of his wife and daughter. It was a painful account, describing the slaughter, the brutality toward captured prisoners, the treachery and cruelty of the *batistianos*.

I wanted to know all about the expedition, from the beginning, and with the help of the newspaper article, conversations with members of the M26-7, and the scant reports that filtered through, I was finally able to get a coherent if incomplete picture of what had happened.

After our arrest and the loss of almost the whole of their supply of arms, the expeditionaries spent the next eight days trying to embark for Cuba, never more than a jump ahead of the police. They had acquired a yacht, the *Gramma,* through an intermediary who had made a down payment in his own name. The plan was to return the yacht to its owner after the landing in Cuba, forfeiting the deposit and liberating the intermediary from his responsibility for the vessel. The *Gramma* was waiting for them in Tuxpan, Veracruz, three hundred miles from Mexico City. It was in need of extensive repairs, which it never received. They did manage to obtain another supply of arms and ammunition, however, before setting out for Tuxpan. The buying of provisions for the trip was left for the last minute. A little after one o'clock on Sunday morning of November 25, both the expeditionaries and the Mexican police reached Tuxpan. Luckily the police were looking for them on the wrong shore, and Fidel Castro and his eighty-one companions were able to set sail for Cuba aboard the dilapidated yacht, whose engine was barely able to function and whose passenger capacity was twenty.

The small yacht, overloaded with men and equipment, made bad time and had constantly to be bailed out. The men were miserable. They had got little sleep during the last frantic week in Mexico, and got little more during the week at sea, unmercifully packed together as they were. The weather was bad and they all were seasick. There was no room to stretch out. In shifts of six hours half of them stood while the other half sat nodding on crossed legs. The supply of water had somehow become polluted with engine fuel, and the last-minute provisions consisted of Hershey bars, oranges, and two hams. On Thursday, land was sighted. It turned out to be Yucatán. They were still in Mexican waters!

Starved, thirsty, exhausted, the expeditionaries finally landed in Cuba early on Sunday of December 2. Fidel ordered the *Gramma* run aground on a swampy coast in Oriente. It was probably in order to annouce his arrival to the Cuban people that Fidel left the vessel stranded in full view of sea, land, and air. The men waded ashore up to their necks in swamp water and mud. They tried to save the equipment by carrying it overhead, but much of it was lost. They had come this far safely because the Batista government, lulled into over-confidence by the news of the successful raid by the Mexican police, had lowered its guard. The relaxation of coastal vigilance had enabled the expeditionaries to slip through, but at sight of the stranded *Gramma,* there was an immediate response by Batista's air force, which strafed and bombed them that same morning. Within three days the expeditionaries fought two encounters with units of the army and gave a good account of themselves.

Unfamiliar with the terrain, the expeditionaries broke up into small groups and straggled toward the Sierra Maestra. The air force continued to strafe them, and dropped leaflets promising to spare their lives if they surrendered. There was sporadic fighting. Most of the expeditionaries, including Cándido, were captured and killed. Their boots torn by the needle-sharp rock the natives call "dog's fangs," their feet bleeding, their tongues swollen from four days of thirst under a burning sun, they staggered helplessly toward the peasant huts scattered over the area where Batista's soldiers lay in wait for them. Despite the leaflets, all but a handful of those who gave themselves up were shot in the act of surrendering. One week after Fidel Castro's fulfillment of his promise to land in Cuba in 1956 most of his valorous, dedicated followers were dead.

A guide named Crescencio Pérez, learning that the report of the expeditionaries' annihilation was false, went in search of the survivors. He found Fidel and eleven others wandering dispersed in the cane fields. The twelve managed to regroup and to find refuge, at last, in the heights of the Sierra Maestra. Two months later Herbert Matthews, of *The New York Times,* published his interview with Fidel, and a photograph, and for the first time we knew for certain that Fidel was alive.

As Melba Hernández de Montané had predicted, there was no general uprising in Cuba. The fighting in Santiago de Cuba was the work of Frank País, whose underground group was the only one to answer the call. It was thanks to Frank País, too, that Fidel, in his first month in the Sierra Maestra, received seventy men, fully equipped. If it had not been for him, Fidel would have remained isolated in the mountains with only eleven harried, ill-equipped men. Frank País was murdered half a year before the victory, and only a month after the slaying of his younger brother.

*   *   *

On my release from prison on bail (I had to report weekly to the police), I decided to stay on in my ample house and put it at the disposition of members of the M26-7. Soon afterwards the lease for the adjacent house expired, and its occupants came to live with me. My new guests, besides Pedro Miret—who from that time on directed the military end of the movement in Mexico—were his wife, Ennio Leyva, and eight other expedition-aries who because of the disruption caused by the arrests had been left behind. Once again my house filled with life, and once again with subversive activity. There were always at least a dozen people living in it, and at one point we were as many as twenty-three; we had to rent other living quarters for the overflow. For, with the Batista dictatorship growing worse day by day, more and more exiles arrived from Cuba to live in Mexico, and the majority were youngsters eager to train as guerrillas and join Fidel Castro in the *sierra*.

Young men I had never seen arrived at my garden gates, suitcase in hand, asking if I lived there. A time came when at the mere sight of a young man with a suitcase, Tere or I or some other one of us ran to open the gate without stopping to ask questions. They identified themselves afterwards. We put them up in my house, or else sent them on to one of the others. One of the boys called my house the "Casuso-Hilton Hotel," because it was larger and better furnished than the others, and had Tere to spoil them, and two maids to perform the domestic chores. When the beds and couches were taken, they slept in sleeping bags or on folded rugs on the floor.

On one occasion a whole group of Cuban schoolboys arrived, all but one of them under eighteen years old. They had run away from the school they had been sent to in Washington, D.C., had bought a car and rifles, which they stashed under the seats, and, with a Cuban flag, an M26-7 pennant, and a picture of Fidel pasted on a window, had crossed the border legally (it never occurred to the frontier guards to suspect them of carrying arms and to look under the seats). Of course my house was under police surveillance and to keep weapons there was out of the question. When those schoolboys proudly informed us that their car outside was filled with arms, I hastily drove it to a friend's house, where we unloaded its dangerous contents. As was to be expected, a couple of weeks later came the "expedition" of the parents— a delegation representing the boys' fathers—whose reasonable, persuasive attitude in the end met with success, and all but the oldest boy, Roberto Roca, went tearfully back to school. Then Roberto's father, an alumnus of the Generation of the Thirties, came to speak to his son. They had a man-to-man talk, and the father all but ended up himself going into training alongside the son. Roberto stayed with us, married a Mexican girl, and some time later went off to Cuba and the Sierra Maestra. By the end of the campaign he held the rank of captain.

We succeeded in setting up a ranch far from the city

and unknown to the police. The boys trained there, and once I went up and spent two of my pleasantest days of that period, sleeping on the floor in a sleeping bag, shooting pistols at a target, climbing mountains with the others. They were good boys, and I came to love them like an older sister, in spite of their rather elemental nature and their inability to talk of anything but guns and their female conquests.

At first we tried sending the young men to Cuba in expeditions. On one small expedition which left by boat from Yucatán almost half the boys were treacherously left behind, for petty, selfish reasons, by some older Cuban politicians who had attached themselves to our group. After many such vexations it was decided that it would be more practical thereafter to send men and munitions by plane, while letting as many as possible enter Cuba individually, to be taken into the *sierra* by elements of the underground.

My comportment during the interrogation at the time of my arrest brought unexpected dividends. The same police officials who had questioned me treated me afterwards with great respect. Not only did I continue to transport arms in an automobile which they knew by sight, but with their help I was able to locate the exiles who were detained. And once, when Fidel made a desperate appeal by underground radio for ten thousand American rifle bullets, one of the police officials put me in contact with smugglers. On introducing me, he gave me the highest recommendation from the point of view of the underworld: "You can deal with her, I can testify that she doesn't talk." The police officials helped me in spite of the fact that after the raid, Batista had sent a gift of $25,000 for them to divide among themselves.

To cripple Batista's sugar harvest, we smuggled phosphorus into Cuba in cans of "sweets." The phosphorus was used to set fire to the plantations. This was by order of Fidel, who set the example by putting his own family's plantation at the top of the list.

One day late in 1957, about a year after the invasion, the boys from one of our houses came to inform me that Fidel's mother had arrived from Cuba. With a rush of emotion I hurried off to see her.

For reasons of discipline and security the boys' living quarters had to be kept very clean, orderly, and quiet. Although they were not at the ranch, they were, nevertheless, in training. They were taught military tactics and judo by a young American veteran of the Korean War. Their "marches" took the form of walks in Chapultepec Forest. It was strictly forbidden to have alcohol on the premises.

The first thing I heard as I drew near the door was the sound of loud laughter and conversation. When the door was opened I saw a circle of boys holding glasses, and a tall, very thin, angular woman with dyed black hair and the general look of a Cuban peasant seated on a chair with a bottle of Bacardi rum beside her. Before we were introduced she took a long drink. The boys told her that I had been of great help to her son in Mexico.

"Ah, yes?" she said indifferently. "As a matter of fact I wanted to go to your house today and talk to you. I have come to Mexico to see you people about the burning of my cane fields. I have just spent twenty-six thousand dollars to have them weeded. I want you, as you are in radio contact with the Sierra Maestra, to arrange to have my sugar crop left alone."

I was more than astonished; I was indignant. While Fidel was risking his life and suffering privations of every kind, her only concern was for her cane fields. Within me a choked voice, wanting to weep, said over and over, "Poor Fidel, poor, unhappy Fidel." I went into the kitchen, not knowing what to say to that woman. In the kitchen, another empty bottle. The house leader came

130

over to me and explained that she had sent for the rum and invited them to drink, and, as she was Fidel's mother . . . I stayed a little longer. The only thing I heard from her was that things were fine for her in Cuba. Army officers dropped in for coffee when they were in her neighborhood. One of them was Cowley, military chief of the city of Holguin. (During Christmas 20 persons were hanged from lamp posts in Holguin.) Thinking of the value she could have as a symbol (and also to spare Fidel her thoughtless behavior in Cuba), I tried to get her to stay on in Mexico, where three of her daughters and her stepdaughter were in exile. But she brushed aside my reasons with the answer:

"I am a Cuban: why shouldn't I return to Cuba?"

She said this before a group of ten boys, all Cubans, who could not return to Cuba legally because they were fighting for Cuba's freedom. I wanted to tell that woman, "And what are these men—Poles? Or do you think they are here because they like it here?" I left without her once having asked me, as so many mothers of the *Gramma* boys asked in their numerous letters to me, how her son had felt while he was in Mexico, how he had lived, what he had done . . . Not a word.

When I arrived home and told Pedro Miret about this meeting, the suppressed desire to cry brought an ache to my throat. I remember that Pedro said, "If it surprised you, it's because you don't know her. That's the way she is."

One day, in a talk with Pedro after his father had died, I learned to my surprise that not only was Fidel's father dead, but that he had died in October 1956. Although I was seeing a lot of Fidel at the time, he had never mentioned it. Then I realized that all the boys had spoken of their fathers except Fidel. Apparently there was some hidden wound relating to his childhood which had never healed. Such disunity within a family is a rare thing

131

in Cuba, a land where consanguineous cohesion and loyalty is its society's most solid foundation; where during economic crises kindred families group together and share what they have; where even friends in need are given succor; where sons and daughters live with their parents until they marry; and where if an aged person ends his days in an asylum, it is because he has nobody in the world, not even a married niece or nephew to give him shelter.

Shortly after meeting his mother, I wrote Fidel a letter, expressing, with an almost maternal tenderness, my faith in our friendship and in his noble mission. It never reached him.

chapter

10

In Cuba, the people began little by little to respond to the movement started by Fidel Castro. Volunteers joined him in the Sierra Maestra as the mountain became the focal point of Cuban hope and faith. The entire civil population of Cuba contributed to the building of Castro into a legendary hero. The peasants of the *sierra* served as messengers, kept Fidel informed of the movements of the army on the plains and shared what little they had with his growing band. In the cities, sabotage increased, secret publications were printed and distributed, bonds were sold, arms and ammunition found their way to the rebel stronghold.

From the beginning of the fighting, civilian resistance and aid to the rebels brought increasingly violent reprisals by the military in the rural areas and by the police in the cities. The army bombed the peasants' huts, using napalm bombs. Their purpose was to clear the Sierra Maestra area and its surroundings so that the rebels would lose all hope of sustenance and aid. Neither the bombings nor the daily hanging of peasants and burning of their huts succeeded in cutting the rebels off from aid, whereupon Batista resorted to the same terrible measure that General Valeriano Weyler had used in the War of Independence: reconcentration. Sick, starving, barefoot *guajiros* and their families, representing almost half the peasant population of Oriente Province, were forced off the land and into the nearby cities and towns to squat on the sidewalks. Such was the revulsion inspired inside and outside Cuba that a few weeks later Batista was forced to countermand the order; but once back in their huts, the peasants continued to be harassed and bombed. Batista obtained those napalm bombs, as well as almost all the rest of his military equipment, from the United States— in the interest of "hemispheric defense." We protested in vain. We presented proof—and even published a photograph of a Cuban army plane being loaded with bombs on the American base at Guantánamo—to no avail. It was only a few months before the fall of Batista, when the cost in human lives of the struggle against the dictator amounted to approximately twenty thousand, that the U.S. government was finally prevailed upon to discontinue selling him war materials.

In the cities, barbarism flourished. Eleuterio Pedraza, the suppressor of the general strike of March 1935, was back—this time at the army helm. After that March strike he had engineered a coup against Batista; when the attempt failed, he had gone into exile. Now, with Batista back and again in need of such men in order to murder Cubans en masse, they reconciled. (The assassins always return, for killing is their only skill. They are like the shark that has tasted human blood.) Every sunrise revealed dozens of corpses hanging from lamp posts or lying crumpled on the pavement. Two girls innocent of any political activity, the Giralt sisters, were ferociously murdered in their home in Havana, their screams sounding through the neighborhood as they were battered to death. The most barbaric methods of torture, not excluding castration, were daily incidents in the police stations, where the groans of a whole generation of youths were heard as they were tortured for information, or for having aided the revolutionary movement. (One such building became so infamous that after the victory it was torn down stone by stone.) An old priest of a Havana suburb died as a result of the beating he received from the police.

Every social class, every occupational group participated in the revolutionary movement. Priests and pastors, professors, lawyers, doctors, skilled and unskilled workers engaged in civic resistance or joined the rebels in the mountains. If the middle and professional classes contributed the most, many of the rich also helped, with money and with shelter for revolutionists wanted by the police. Individually the workers too contributed a great deal, despite the fact that working conditions in Cuba were the best in Latin America. If they could not do much as a unit it was because their unions were controlled by men in Batista's pay and there was nobody to organize them. The leaders of the M26-7 did not know how to organize on the working-class level, and the Communists, who did, remained aloof from the "bourgeois movement" until the last six or seven months, when they began to see that it was gathering momentum. The struggle could have been considerably shortened if the Communists had co-operated on the two occasions that Fidel called for a general strike. But they did not, and both strikes failed. The second, in April 1958, left us crushed and discouraged.

Groups unrelated to the M26-7 were active in the revolution. The Revolutionary Directorate, for example, in addition to making its suicidal attack on the presidential palace, established its own front in the Sierra del Escambray. And if the M26-7 in the United States was able to get several expeditions through to Cuba despite Uncle Sam's vigilance, it was thanks largely to the donations made by Carlos Prío, who was a member of the political party called the Cuban Revolutionary Party (the *auténticos*). Prío's efforts on behalf of the revolution, incidentally, caused him to be detained in ignominious fashion (he was handcuffed and made to walk to the police station) in Miami. This one action cost the United States a good deal of prestige in Latin America.

Without all this help from the different classes and organized groups of Cuban society, Fidel never could have won his fight. In contrast to Batista's well-equipped, well-supplied army of thirty-five thousand men, the rebel force at no time numbered more than a thousand. On the other hand, Fidel would have won much more quickly if Batista had not had the moral and material support of the United States. With a shorter war, the figure of Fidel Castro would very likely never have swelled to the gigantic dimensions which it acquired in proportion as the Cuban people suffered and despaired. Fidel was only one of the factors in our national life. It was not necessary for him to be made into a god, and the master of the whole country. Once again, the United States is paying the price of its short-sightedness.

*　　*　　*

Fidel established a rigid discipline among his men. Any rebel whom he considered to be an informer was executed. I know of at least one case that was very doubtful. (And from what I have recently seen of the executions of his former companions, my doubts have increased.) He also hanged or shot peasants who gave information to the army. Shortly after he and his band left Mexico, I learned that he had used a room in one of the expeditionary houses as a jail. Such a thing is perfectly reasonable; soldiers need discipline; but I also heard that one of his men had been shot. In fairness to Fidel, I was never able to learn the young man's name, or to check the truth of the story. But the rumor was a persistent one among the later recruits, who said that the man had completely vanished and that letters had come from his family asking why he did not write. And Pedro's denials patently

136

lacked conviction. I only heard these things later, while Fidel was in the Sierra Maestra, but they worried me a great deal. His terrible inflexibility, the obsession for arms and militias that they all had, and those olive-green uniforms made me fear that the movement might degenerate into something of a fascistic nature—the "Olive-Green Shirts." Many Cuban intellectuals, as I discovered, shared my anxiety.

On Fidel's orders, however, no military prisoners were ever executed, but were liberated instead. This policy won for him a reputation of generosity and nobility in war and encouraged the opposing troops to refuse to fight against him. As time went on, Batista's soldiers and officers began to desert in increasing numbers. As a warrior Fidel had the spectacular qualities necessary to capture the imagination of the people. In addition to his courage, he was a cunning commander. He has the gift of remarkable astuteness where the furthering of his aims is concerned. He once fooled Herbert Matthews into thinking the rebel army bigger than it was. At a time when he had only seventy men, he took Matthews past groups of men who immediately ran through short cuts to reappear in another part of the woods, changing a hat or a shirt as they ran. (Fidel told about this at the Overseas Press Club luncheon in New York.) But his most outstanding quality is his intuition. Those who fought beside him in the *sierra* have told me how, going from one place to another in the middle of the forest, he would suddenly stop and say, "No—not through there." They would change direction and go by a round-about route, and learn afterwards that near those very places where Fidel had stopped—"as if struck by lightning," his comrades said —there had been enemy troops lying in ambush. This happened not once but several times. Be it intuition, magic, a "lucky star," or whatever, there is a quality in the man that warns him of danger and that attracts men to him—and even, apparently, birds. When he entered the Columbia Military Camp for the first time, after the fall of Batista, and made his first speech to Cuba, a flock of doves was let into the air as a symbol of peace and liberty. The doves flew around him and then one alighted on his shoulder and stayed there during the entire long speech. (Thereafter he appeared on post cards and in paintings with the dove on his shoulder.)

The strange incident was repeated—and this time I witnessed it—during our visit to Washington in April 1959, when he paid a visit to the Lincoln Memorial. Fidel stood for a while in silent contemplation before the statue of that great American for whom he always said he had the greatest esteem. From a neighboring park a number of doves flew toward the monument, and one of them settled on Lincoln's hand for a few moments, then flew directly to Fidel's shoulder, exactly as the one in the Columbia Camp had done. The Cuban photographers, having witnessed the occurrence twice and in such totally different places, were astounded. One said to me, "Look, I've got goose pimples—if I hadn't seen it I would never have believed it."

Against such personal magnetism there is, at first sight, no resistance possible. It has caused many foreign writers and journalists interviewing him to be converted into rabid *fidelistas*.

At first I was a *fidelista,* and a very sincere one—even after the blinders came off my eyes—because of the affection, esteem, and sympathy I conceived for this man, who without, finally, being an Atlas, carried on his shoulders a world that was much too big for them. That world was heavy enough when it implied the leadership of the anti-Batista movement; it grew even heavier when it represented glory and adoration as complete as any man can know; and it crashed to the ground with the addition of the heaviest burden of all for the shoulders of a warrior—peace.

It was after Fidel's second attempt to incite a general strike failed that the Communists added their support to the movement. This was in May 1958. Meanwhile the fighting went on. Few battles were fought in the mountains. The army never went up to fight, but contented itself with trying to eliminate Fidel in an occasional ambush. Sometimes the rebels descended to hunt for arms and ammunition. There were frequent skirmishes, and on three or four occasions they managed to surprise a provisional army post and replenish their scant arsenal.

In the fall of 1957 there was a mutiny of the navy in the port of Cienfuegos. The townspeople joined in the rebellion, and declared their allegiance to the revolutionary movement. Then Batista had the city bombed, and a large part of the population was wiped out. The precise number of dead was never determined, for the army, using bulldozers, quickly buried them in open ditches.

Toward the end of 1958, Che Guevara and Camilo Cienfuegos went down from the Sierra Maestra with a group of men and, repeating part of the historic Invasion route traced by "the Titan" in the War of Independence, got as far as Santa Clara, the capital of the central province of Las Villas. They entered the city on Christmas Day. Batista ordered the city bombed, as he had done the year before to Cienfuegos. Again part of a city was destroyed. But Batista knew it was all over. His soldiers and officers were deserting in great numbers. American aid had been officially discontinued. Sabotage was widespread. His tyranny was hated throughout the island. There were four rebel fronts harassing his dwindling, unenthusiastic army from their strongholds in the Sierra Maestra, the Sierra del Escambray, the Sierra Cristal, and in Pinar del Río. He now did what Jefferson Caffery had not let him do in the general strike of 1935, during his first dictatorship: he fled the country.

He left the reins of government in the hands of a Junta. But the Junta was fated to govern only a few hours, for in Santiago de Cuba, Fidel Castro immediately declared Manuel Urrutia President of the Republic. Manuel Urrutia, as one of the magistrates at the trial of a young rebel captured after the Moncada assault, in 1953, had said in his decision: "The tyranny of Batista is illegitimate. Therefore a rebellion against that tyranny is legitimate, and must not be punished." The rebel was Fidel Castro.

* * *

Batista took refuge in the Dominican Republic, with his colleague Trujillo. He left behind a country economically ruined, with a treasury that was practically empty. It is estimated that he carried off $600 million of the country's money.

On the day Batista fell, Fidel—for what reason I do not know—called for a general strike. Possibly it was in order to demonstrate his power. Or it may be, as it is one of Fidel's peculiarities that he must always find some way to "even the score," that he was thinking of the two times he had asked for a general strike in vain. The work stoppage lasted three days, and instead of invigorating the country, it paralyzed it. What satisfaction the new "maximum leader" can have derived from it, I cannot imagine. In the end he had to call the strike off, as a result of the popular clamor demanding facilities for the celebrations.

At length Fidel's triumphal caravan reached Havana. His first speech, at a moment in which he was surrounded by universal adoration and acclaim, was strangely haunted with death. In that speech, with the dove

140

perched on his shoulder and unaccustomed victory converging upon him from a throng of worshipful faces, he named his brother as his successor. It was as if his thoughts were lingering, not on the dead from whom he had arisen, but on death itself.

* * *

When Pedro Miret, his wife, and the other expeditionaries who had not sailed with the *Gramma* came to live in my house, the landlady gave me an ultimatum to the effect that either I throw out those Cubans or I would have to get out myself. The lawsuit dragged on more than a year, and I lost it in April 1958, just before the second general strike failed. I was given three days to vacate the house. I sold everything and watched strangers carrying off my memory-filled furniture, devalued by two years of constant wear and tear, for next to nothing. I took a room in a rooming house. I had to ship my three dogs to my parents in Cuba; a week after their arrival, "Tosco," my beloved champion springer spaniel, was dead— poisoned by the *batistianos*. Shortly afterwards Pedro Miret, on a flight to the Sierra Maestra from Costa Rica delivering arms to Fidel, had his landing gear broken and was unable to return. That left me as the intermediary between our boys and the influential Mexicans who were helping us. The boys were disgusted at still being in Mexico, and we set about organizing a very large aerial expedition, which was intended to leave secretly from an airport in Michoacán. To obtain military equipment, I had to make another trip to Miami, and again Carlos Prío gave us a good sum of money. As I had done earlier that year, when I had gone to New York to speak at the meeting at which Dr. Urrutia was declared Provisional President, I sandwiched the trip between the weekly visits to court I was still obliged to make.

141

My rooming house was a dark, sad place. The boys in the houses hardly ever came to see me any more. Those war-minded youngsters resented having a woman for their chief, and especially having to admit dependence upon her. Consequently, they went off on the Michoacán expedition, after I had done so much to set it up, without letting me know. It turned out badly, and they sent for me to help get them out of jail. It happened that they were captured by a general who was an uncle of my ex-husband, and who thought very highly of me. But it was too late for me to do anything: the arms had already been brought in and inventoried. Every time I felt hurt by something those boys had done, I would think of the one good friend I still had in the *sierra,* of Fidel. And every day I begged God not to let anything happen to him.

I started a small academy in which exiled professors were able to give other, more modest exiles than my impulsive and inconsiderate expeditionaries a little education in the form of history and an examination of Cuba's problems. I also joined with some professors in starting a newspaper called *Metas* (*Goals*), concerned with Cuba's future, with post-revolutionary reconstruction and good government. I wrote mainly on the topics which have increasingly preoccupied me since that time: the responsible use of freedom, our psychology, and our national character.

Thus, amid struggles and disappointments, and subsisting on the translations I continued to do for publishing houses, I watched the year of 1958 draw to a close. The rebels were in Santa Clara, and the city was under heavy bombardment by the Batista forces. On New Year's Eve I did not care to go anywhere. Seated in my dismal room, I stayed up all night, unable to sleep. At midnight I leaned out the window. It looked out on a gray wall, but up above, at the edge of a flat roof, there was a little piece of sky. At that moment, marking the entrance of a new year, I could only say to God:

"How much longer, Lord!"

I returned to my armchair and sat there in a kind of reverie. Hours later, at about five in the morning, the hall phone rang. I answered it myself. The call was for me, from Miami. Batista had fallen.

It was not the first time we had received such a report. It had always proven false. Calmly I looked up the numbers of the international-news agencies. No answer at the AP. I called the UP—a name that evoked a kind of trauma in me ever since the McCarthy horror. Ironically, it was this agency that confirmed the incredible, wonderful report of Batista's downfall. A cordial employee read me several cables after I told him my name. I asked him whether I could go there and see them with my own eyes, and was told yes.

With a strange serenity, feeling not the slightest emotion, I made a series of phone calls. Two M26–7 officials did not answer their phones. (It was dawn of New Year's Day!) I called the Cuban embassy. No answer. Then I tried the cultural attaché, a painter friend of mine from the old days. He told me the ambassador was in Cuba. He gave me the number of the *chargé d'affaires,* who answered his phone and made no objection when I told him that I would be at the embassy in an hour and expected it to be officially handed over to me.

I bathed, put on my best dress, one that was left over from more prosperous days. It was drizzling, and I took my umbrella and left that cold, disagreeable room without knowing that I was never to return to it. My life of ups and downs was about to make another full, dizzying turn. There was not a cab or a soul in sight. I walked to the UP offices, eight blocks away, and took that snarl of ticker tape in both hands. I could not believe what my eyes read —details of Batista's flight, the names of those who had

143

fled with him, names as familiar as they were accursed. The employee let me take the cablegrams with me when I told him that I needed proof because the embassy was not yet informed of the development.

I found a cab, and the somnolent driver let me off at the embassy, which takes up half a block and stands in the middle of a large garden, surrounded by a high spiked fence. There had been a time when this building had been like my own house to me. Now I was returning, but instead of satisfaction, I felt only a kind of sad emptiness. Nothing seemed to affect me any more. I was accustomed to winning and losing, to rising and falling unexpectedly.

I wanted to occupy the embassy as early in the day as possible in order to avoid its being attacked and burned by the exiles, for this was what they had absurdly been planning to do when the long-awaited day came. The building and all that it contained was the property of the Republic of Cuba. Someone had to keep it functioning, preferably someone familiar with its inner workings, as I was. Above all, it had to be kept intact.

The doorman, a Cuban over seventy years old, greeted me as he had done every morning for several years, and in the most natural manner, as if I had just been there the day before. "Good morning, señorita," he said, and immediately opened the door for me. The peculiar thing about it was that he had no idea Batista had fallen. I was returning "home," and to him it all seemed perfectly natural.

The first thing I did was ask the Mexican policeman on duty there (I also knew him from the old days) to leave, and to tell his superiors not to send others, I would take the responsibility for keeping order. I knew how much excitement would soon be unleashed, and I felt that it should be kept among ourselves. I asked the doorman to wake the servant in charge of the flag and to have it raised to full mast. Then I ordered the gates to be locked.

The old house was dark and deserted. As I went up the steps from the vestibule I began to emerge from the numbed, unemotional serenity in which I had been moving. I remembered my friends, and with me as I went up those steps that morning went Fidel, Cándido, Miguelito, Pedro . . . those who lived and those who had died; my close friends by virtue of a common struggle. I turned on lights. I illuminated the whole house. Silver-framed portraits of Batista and his wife in evening attire stood on tables in the huge drawing room. In each, his chest was covered with ribbons and decorations. I put them all face down. Then I sat in a large armchair, holding my mass of ticker tape, looking at the expanse of that ghostly room. Quietly I contemplated the emptiness, trying vainly to fill the vacuity within me because instead of joy I felt only a hollow disconsolateness, almost bitterness. It was the hour of victory, but I could think only of those who could no longer see it, and who had innocently given their lives for this day.

A woman came, a friend of the ambassador's wife. I admired her loyalty. She had come to ask permission to take her friend's things. I let her go up with a few suitcases, and she carried off what she wished from the closets —the mink coat, the clothes, the silver picture frames that she assured me were the personal property of the ambassador. Meanwhile her husband arrived. He was a Cuban resident of Mexico and I had known him since before the dictatorship had separated us into opposite camps. I asked him to leave quickly, for the exiles would not be long in arriving and I could not answer for the safety of one who had accepted an honorary post in the Batista government. Then I started to think more concretely of how to avoid unnecessary violence and the sacking of the embassy. The gates could not be kept locked indefinitely, and in any case I could not deny my fellow exiles entry to property that was as much theirs as it was mine. I went from room to room and from office to office gathering up all the Batista effigies and symbols, and had a servant pile them up in the garden.

When the *chargé d'affaires* arrived, we drew up a document by means of which the embassy was officially transferred to me "in the name of the Revolutionary Government headed by Dr. Manuel Urrutia Lleo." Although at that moment the Cuban government was represented, technically, by the Junta, I by-passed the Junta in favor of the Revolutionary Government. (Adolfo López Mateos had just taken office as President of Mexico, and when Urrutia moved into the presidential palace on January 5, his government had already been recognized by that of Mexico since four o'clock that afternoon. It was the first one in the world to do so.)

We had no sooner finished signing the document and its copies when I heard a great uproar at the garden gates. A hysterical mass of exiles was gathered there; some were trying to scale the gates. I went out with the Act and read it to them. I explained that that territory was now a part of free Cuba and our own property, and that they should take care of it as such. I pointed to the pile of Batista's pictures, banners, and trophies, and announced that it was all there, the whole hated past, and would be burned publicly when all the exiles were present. Then, in the name of free Cuba, I myself opened the gates and welcomed them to their house.

There were all kinds of people in that crowd. In addition to our young expeditionaries, there were a good many adventurers who had joined in at the last moment, as usually happens in such cases; but there were also many with horrible burns and scars and mutilations which had been inflicted in the police stations of Cuba, and there was a general air of disappointment that they could not take revenge in some way for what they had suffered.

I went three days without so much as lying down. Six

hundred exiles surrounded me night and day asking when they could leave, each telling me the problem that made his particular case require immediate attention. I put through phone calls to whatever place in Cuba I could think of that might send me passenger or transport planes. But those were the first days of the victory, Fidel had asked the country to stop work while his caravan stopped at every village along our central highway, and the island was without government or services of any kind. Not until the third day did planes of Cubana Airlines begin to arrive. Later, military transports also came, and I had my first contact with the irresponsibility and disorder which characterize the present government of Cuba. Those military planes landed on Mexican soil without warning and without having asked the necessary permission. The pilots who jumped out of them were in rebel dress and thought, apparently, that the whole world must be the same as Cuba. The complaints I received from the Chief of Mexican Aviation grew more and more vigorous. But the pilots' insensate behavior continued despite the innumerable phone calls I made to Cuba asking to be advised of all Mexico-bound flights, so that I might obtain the permission required. Such conduct might have been understandable at the beginning, but its exasperating persistence greatly compromised my work at the embassy vis-à-vis the Mexican authorities.

In answer to a friendly plea by the Mexican government, I disarmed the young, over-excited exiles, almost all of whom were equipped with large pistols. In spite of their cockiness they handed over their weapons one by one, in return for a signed receipt, and the embassy safe filled with arms. It was my fate, it seemed, to store weapons of war! This, however, was only one of the diverse and incongruous activities with which my position of "de facto" ambassador involved me. One day, while I was making my rounds to keep an eye on the six hundred ex-

147

iles who had installed themselves in the embassy until they could be repatriated, I even found myself preventing an execution. As I passed the stairway leading to the basement, I heard what sounded like the cocking of gun hammers. When I went down, I was greeted by the sight of a man standing against a wall and two of our boys aiming pistols at him. The man was a Mexican who had once swindled us in an arms deal and had been foolish enough to appear at the embassy in order to congratulate us on Batista's fall. With all the other problems I already had, all I needed was to have a dead man in the basement— and a Mexican in the bargain! Fortunately, the executioners accepted my authority and my reasoning, and I took the man out of there. I escorted him through the parlor, which was full of Cubans and Mexican reporters who had no idea of what had taken place. Once on the street, I warned him that I could not be responsible for his safety if the boys ever caught him again, and watched until he was out of sight. He did not run, but walked away as if nothing had happened. (Mexicans do not run, just as they do not shout. In anger their voices grow quieter, in danger their faces grow a shade paler, and that is all. His refusal to beg for mercy or to give excuses had saved his life; it had made the "executioners" hesitate long enough to give me time to get there.)

I had time for nothing outside my official labors, and a friend of mine went to my room and moved my things to the embassy. In twenty-four hours my life had made an about-face. I lived in a mansion. The embassy's limousine and a uniformed, protocol-conscious chauffeur took me on the indispensable official calls. The press, which previously had turned its back on us, or openly attacked us, showered me with praise. There were hundreds of calls from acquaintances who in two years had not bothered to call on me or even to phone. Daily over a thousand persons came to congratulate me and to ask me if I needed anything. Ambassadors came to pay their respects. Piles of telegrams and flowers poured in. Formerly inaccessible newspaper and television reporters now asked for interviews. Headlines made much of the fact that I had taken the embassy alone and with no other weapon than an umbrella. (In the old days I suppose an umbrella would have had to be added to the family coat of arms!)

A committee was created to keep order in the embassy, but it was almost impossible in the face of six hundred mutinous exiles who all wished to be the very first to leave. I got the offices functioning. For the post of provisional consul I called on an exile with consular experience. Ten employees were not enough to handle the mounting requests for visas to Cuba. At the same time I had my hands full trying to liberate the former expeditionaries still imprisoned in Michoacán and to recover the costly load of arms that had been seized in the fiasco. When I made my trip to court that week (I was still awaiting trial) I was accompanied by a flock of reporters. As for the two others who had been arrested with me, Pedro Miret, of course, was in Cuba, and Ennio Leyva was one of those whom my "uncle," the general, had imprisoned in Michoacán. The day after the President of Mexico bypassed protocol and invited me to participate as a representative of Cuba in the New Year greetings which he customarily receives from the diplomatic corps, the judge threw out the indictment against Pedro, Ennio, and me, declaring that there was no crime to prosecute. Ennio, however, remained in the Michoacán jail.

The only thing I received with promptness and efficiency from Cuba was a series of horrible photographs of dead men who had been murdered and tortured and mutilated unbelievably by the Batista people. Using these, I launched a campaign in Mexico on my own account, exposing the brutality of the Batista government, before the campaign was ever begun in Cuba with the

149

name of "Operation Truth." In a special press conference I released the photographs along with a detailed account of what the Cuban people had suffered. Up to the very end of the *batistato* the majority of Mexican newspaper editors had persistently refused to believe the stories of that barbarity.

On the twenty-fifth day after I had taken over the embassy the last Cuban revolutionary still in Mexico, Ennio Leyva, was released as a personal favor to me, and on the twenty-sixth I left that country with Ennio and his wife and their little son. The embassy was functioning smoothly; the six hundred exiles had been repatriated and with them I had sent Gabriela and Alfonsina, the two humble Mexican women who for two years had helped us and given the exiles so much motherly care and affection. (Later I was to regret having sent them, when I learned that Fidel did not take the trouble to receive them.) I also sent poor "Colonel" Bayo, who had wandered about the embassy like a lost soul because he had not been sent for from Cuba. I made him think he probably *had* been sent for but that the communication had gone astray, and that what he ought to do was go straight to the Habana-Hilton, where Fidel had installed himself, and once there he would be set right. He went, and it turned out well.

The day I left, Tere, my beloved cook who had come to look after me at the embassy, brought a *mariachi* band to the embassy garden to see me off with "Las Golondrinas," the Mexican song of farewell. She and her children, whom I had watched grow up in my house in Chapultepec Heights, presented me with a last gift, an orchid. That day, for the first time since the overthrow of Batista, I was able to cry as I said good-by to Mexico.

chapter

11

In Mexico, Fidel had told me that as soon as we won I should take the first plane to Cuba. But I was at the Habana-Hilton Hotel two days, staying a few floors below that of Fidel, before I was able to see him. I spent those two days waiting in the anteroom. I sat in front of a door on the other side of which was my friend, whose voice I could hear whenever someone went in or out—the voice of the man who had lived in my house as if it were his own.

To be refused entry by new guards with submachine guns, impressive men with beards who were complete strangers to me and who treated me as if I myself were some stranger, was a painful and bitter experience. But a stranger I was. Much had happened since Fidel had left Mexico. The earlier period had been overshadowed. I tried to understand, and to be patient. Sadly I looked for a familar face, for a survivor from the Mexico days among all those uniformed men swarming through the hotel. I realized once again that almost all the old ones were gone, and I felt the blow afresh, as if I were learning the fact of their death for the first time.

I found out that in order to get through to Fidel I would have to make contact with Celia Sánchez. Celia Sánchez was a small, thin young woman of indefinite age, with black hair, sharp features, and a slow, deliberate manner. When Fidel had been in the Sierra Maestra only a few weeks she had come to offer her services to him as a guide. Her father was a doctor on a sugar plantation near the Sierra Maestra, and she was familiar with those mountains, in which she and a group of girls had often gone exploring. In addition, as a member of the M26-7 since a few months before the *Gramma* expedition, she had carefully studied her native locale in case Fidel should land there—as he did. She had spent the two hard revolutionary years at Fidel's side as his aide-de-camp, personally supervising his meals. She also performed quartermaster duties, giving every man his arms and provisions. As their number increased, the labors were divided, but she remained Fidel's closest assistant. She was at his side when the triumphal caravan made its way through the island, and in the Hilton she continued to concern herself with Fidel's personal well-being.

When I met her, knowing with what devotion she had cared for him during those two years, I thanked her for all that she had done. I always felt an affectionate esteem for her, and she never showed me the slightest hostility. I find it very hard to believe what some people have since told me—that she tried to alienate me from Fidel. I think that even before we met she knew of my devotion to him, that it was of a purely fraternal nature, and that whatever I did to help him was innocent of any other kind of personal feeling. Moreover, in all the time I worked for Fidel I was very careful not to trespass onto her territory, which in any case did not interest me. Our duties vis-à-vis Fidel were of different kinds and did not overlap. She was, and is, the closest to him, giving him her unqualified approval and devotion in all he does. Of all those around him, it is she who enjoys his greatest confidence.

On the third morning I at last found myself inside the presidential suite on the twenty-third floor of the Habana-Hilton, a suite that was in the process of becoming famous. There was another wait—bearded men in uniform wandered about the place or stood talking—and finally Celia bade me enter Fidel's room. As the door was opened, I caught sight of Fidel, bearded and in uniform like the others, pacing up and down as he gave orders to four or five members of the rebel army. The only one I recognized was Che Guevara. I noticed acutely the absence of Cándido at his side—a ghostly void. It was the first time I had ever seen Fidel preparing an action of any kind without him.

Fidel stopped, returned my emotional embrace as matter-of-factly as if he had seen me only the day before, and said to me, "Don't go. Wait." And he went on with what he was doing. A little chilled, I sat down in the only available place—his very wide, unmade bed—while he continued pacing and giving orders to one of his lieutenants.

"Go to the Sierra Maestra," he said, "and order all the cattle rounded up! Make the storekeepers toe the line." He turned with a sweeping gesture of his long arm and added, "We're going to ruin all those merchants!" He had a fierce, almost insane expression on his face that I had never seen before. Then he turned to me with a tragic grimace which since then has been his equivalent for a smile. He was seeking my approval.

I think I must have been staring at him with pain and astonishment, because he turned back brusquely to the others. Immediately adopting a pleasant and lively manner, he finished giving the men their instructions. For me it was a shock to see that his experience in the mountains, and his subsequent triumph, had made him arrogant. Arrogance, indeed, became his chief personality trait. Though at times he was able to simulate humility convincingly when it was necessary, he soon came to tolerate nothing less than unqualified admiration. In those few moments I understood that the past two years had not matured and improved him as I had hoped. On the contrary; he had gone the other way: the Fidel I had known was as dead as Cándido.

I went to the balcony with the excuse of looking out at the fine view of the city. I suppose I felt the need to find greatness somewhere. Guevara, who himself is neither rustic nor rough, must have understood my sadness and loneliness, for he came over and greeted me with a friendly smile, putting his hand on my shoulder. Thereafter, though we rarely had the opportunity to converse (neither he nor Raúl Castro had to wait in the anteroom before seeing Fidel; in this they were the exception), he always greeted me in the same friendly way as he passed by.

Once the others had left, Fidel listened in a distracted way to the few brief sentences in which I summarized the recent happenings in Mexico, and my reasons for not coming sooner. As I spoke I noticed that he had altered physically: in addition to the beard, he now had a paunch, appeared to be flabby, and his teeth had gone bad during his two years in the Sierra Maestra. When I expressed my desire to be of service to him, he told me that many foreign newspapermen were wandering about in the lobby, waiting to see him, and that I should attend to them. Celia, who had re-entered the room, thought it was a good idea, and Fidel, feeling more animated and close to me now, added that I should move to his floor, and told Celia to take care of it. He wanted me to start in right away. As I left, I heard him tell someone that he would be there that evening to receive callers.

Celia's room was in Fidel's suite, and there, where I met two of her sisters, both as friendly and delicate as she, we learned that there was a room available across the hall on the same floor, which had been set aside for those nearest "the Chief." To get to that floor, one had to pass two guard posts, and the elevator men took no one to that floor who had not first been authorized by the guard.

154

I went to the room and met an officer just coming out of it. He wore the same uniform as the others, but there the resemblance between him and the rebels ended. He was clean-shaven, his bearing was martial, his appearance neat and clean. He was Captain Jesús Yanes Pelletier, Fidel's personal aide and the former Batista army officer who had saved Fidel's life by refusing to poison him when Fidel was in prison at Santiago de Cuba after the Moncada assault. After having been freed in the general amnesty of 1955, he had gone into exile in the United States, and had helped the revolutionary movement by obtaining arms and sending them to the Sierra Maestra. At the time I knew nothing of all this, but that tall, elegant mulatto with his fine features, bright smile, and the manners of a well-raised, considerate man presented a sharp contrast to all those bearded men with their alarming, matted locks and inexperience in dealing with people. I liked him at once. Yanes informed me that the room had just been assigned to him, but that he would give it to me if I wished. I thought of how much trouble it was to get to that floor, what with the guards below and Fidel's personal escort above, and I realized that, although it might be a very special honor to live on Fidel Castro's exclusive floor, I would not have much independence of movement or be able to receive friends freely. I decided I could do without the special honor, and kept the room I had.

Back in my room, I got in touch with the telephone operators of the Hilton and advised them that from then on I would be taking care of any foreigners wishing to see Fidel, especially those of the press. The telephone girls were as clever as they were charming and friendly. They were almost a part of that errant government in that they knew everything that was going on, and the one I talked to that morning told me of the most urgent case —Jack Paar. Discouraged after a week of useless waiting,

Paar had gone to the airport to return to the United States. I asked her to connect me with the airport, and got through to him just as he was about to board the plane. I persuaded him to come back to the Hilton, and assured him that his request to film a television interview with Fidel that same evening would be granted.

Paar returned and I took him to Fidel's suite, but he was out. The constant traffic and military vigilance in the suite made it difficult to set aside any one of the rooms for technicians and equipment, and Paar took the suite below, on floor twenty-two, and, relying completely on my word, started getting everything ready. I had heard Fidel say he would be at the Hilton that night and thought it would be a simple matter for him to go down for a few minutes and have his interview with Paar. I was pleased to have this as my first task, for I knew the program and was aware of its popularity in America. I thought it could do us a lot of good at a time when the American press was already beginning to attack us. Fidel returned to the Hilton half an hour before the time I had arranged for the interview, and I went to tell him that we were starting out with a fine opportunity.

I found his suite filled with disorder, tension, and irritability. This, I was to discover, was the atmosphere in which Fidel had moved since victory. It was the atmosphere of unsureness in everything. One could never be certain of what was coming, or whether he would show up for an appointment. He was our temperamental "prima donna." In the mornings Celia would give me the "weather forecast" of his humor for the day; almost always it was "stormy."

I spoke to Celia first, and was told, to my amazement, that Fidel would not do the Paar interview under any circumstances. "He has had enough of the Americans and their way of twisting everything he says," she said, without giving me a chance to point out that on this program

156

he would be speaking directly to his audience, without intermediaries. Fidel came out of his room, with that hurried, distracted air of his as if he were being blown along by a tornado. He too refused to hear me. I tried to talk to him while he paced through the drawing room, but he did not let me finish. With mortifying indifference and lack of consideration he said to me in a brutally slow and quiet tone, "Go down and tell the gentleman I will not do the program."

"But, Fidel—"

"In fact I won't be here. Let's go!" he barked to his personal escort in a sudden change of tempo. The escort sprang up, seizing their rifles and submachine guns, then waited for him as he dashed back into his room. I went out into the corridor. I was so disconcerted and miserable that I did not know what to do next. I could not go down and deliver that message and give the impression of children playing games. It occurred to me that no position of official responsibility in Cuba at that moment could be taken seriously, and mine least of all. I leaned up against the wall with my head in my arms, trying frantically to think of something to say to him when he came out so that he would reconsider, knowing that only a few seconds were left before a catastrophe took place, wishing the earth would swallow me up. At that moment I decided to go away and give up trying to work with Fidel. Just then a smiling voice—that was its texture—asked me what was the matter. It was Captain Yanes, who had just stepped from the elevator. I explained rapidly. Yanes had lived in the United States. He knew the show, and the criticism that was in store for us if the program did not go on. He told me not to budge, and went inside with his light, cheerful step. Of all those around Fidel he was the only one who did not live under chronic tension, and who knew how to smile. The others, without exception, had changed into the "angry young men" of the revolution—slovenly, grimy, unsmiling, in love with excess.

A few minutes later I heard the muffled sounds of the escort—dry sounds, like those of a funeral procession—and the great door of the presidential suite opened. The escort, with Fidel in the middle, emerged with its air of clearing the way. Fidel was wearing that new stubborn expression of his, as if the disagreeable and confused atmosphere inside his suite had left its stamp on his face. Without a break in his hard, headlong stride he said to me, as I hastened after him, "I'm going to do it, but don't get me into any more of these things." He spoke in a low voice, as he always did to me, and with visible annoyance. But it was not me he was angry at. It was the Americans. That afternoon he had read some articles in American newspapers and magazines attacking "Operation Truth."

Yanes won my gratitude and friendship that day. The program turned out well. Fidel, seated between Jack Paar and me, was his "other self," sociable, friendly, and those who saw us on that television show could never have guessed that as soon as it was over his face would resume its grim, frowning expression. Never again did I arrange anything for Fidel without his prior and reiterated approval.

Fidel had cause to be angry, for the offensive of hostile attacks launched by the American press in January of 1959 were already worsening the relations between our two countries. The mentality which fears that a revolution may affect its investments began instinctively to attack us in several American publications even before we took the measures which did affect them. One of the first measures we did take, "Operation Truth," did not affect U.S. interests, but it furnished a handy target for hostile elements in the American press.

"Operation Truth" was the fulfillment of a promise made to the people of Cuba. According to that promise

158

the murderers and torturers of twenty thousand victims were to be publicly tried, with the sentences to be imposed and carried out by the revolutionary tribunals instead of by the relatives of those victims. After Bastista's downfall the Cuban people did not give itself up to vengeance, as it had after the fall of Machado. There was not a single lynching. The people were confident that the Revolutionary Government would carry out its promise to punish the guilty. The trials were held in the public place in Havana that could accommodate the most spectators. Everybody was allowed to attend those trials, or they could be watched on television. Witnesses appeared, sentences were delivered, justice was meted out. Certainly it was an extremely unpleasant episode, cruel and hard. But what else was there to do? Even the Roman Catholic Church understood and defended "Operation Truth."

But the American press attacked it fiercely, calling the trials a "circus." It spoke of "rivers of blood." What had it said about the innocent blood that was spilled by Batista and his team of killers? Moral censure of the punishment is hardly justified when the preceding crime is met only with indifference and silence. If a public vendetta had been permitted in Cuba, it would have been a very different matter. The whole world would then have seen an atrocious spectacle—the avenging of twenty thousand individual murders. If the trials had been held in private, the tribune's intention to punish the accused might have become suspect, as well as the very integrity of the trials, and the sentences.

At Machado's overthrow the guilty were pardoned. The Tribunals of Sanctions that were created did not inflict capital punishment. And many of the Machado murderers, as a result, reappeared in the two Batista dictatorships to apply their old skills. These were socially unredeemable men who had lost human contact and become blood-lusting beasts. One does not enjoy exterminating roaches or mosquitos or poisonous animals, yet they must be exterminated, despite the fact that they, unlike humans, are unaware of the harm they do. The execution of some—only *some;* many were imprisoned, or exiled—of the cutthroats who killed and tortured so many Cubans of both sexes was an unavoidable post-war phenomenon. The American press, it seemed, no longer wished to remember the Nuremberg trials, but was eager to call those in Havana a "bloodbath"—a term which for some reason was never used to describe the Batista regime. The U.S. press, therefore, played its part in Castro's alliance with the Soviet bloc.

I am sure that Fidel Castro was not a Communist in January of 1959. Nor had he any intention of embracing communism. It is true that his obsession with destruction, hatred, and retaliation would select communism as the system best suited to accommodate him, but there can be no doubt that he was pushed into its arms. At his first foreign press conference, when he declared that he was thinking of introducing laws in favor of the poorest segment of the population, one reporter remarked, "So, then, Dr. Castro, this could be called a social revolution." "No," Fidel explained, "this is only a democratic revolution." Such, at least at that time, were his ideas on the subject. But it became increasingly difficult to dissuade the U.S. press from its preconceived notion. I remember that in Havana the American correspondents would repeatedly ask Fidel the classic question: "How do you think our conflicts with Cuba can be resolved?" And his reply was always the same, sometimes with despair: "Understanding. And you must stop *lying!*"

Far from being annoyed with me over the Paar affair, Fidel paid me an unexpected tribute. The very next day, as he reclined in his favorite striped pajamas listening to my recent experiences in Mexico, in a relatively tranquil moment, he suddenly called the Minister of Foreign Affairs, and in his most correct manner asked, as his first formal, government favor, that I be appointed ambassador-at-large. He said it was owed me in recognition of all that I had done, and gone through, as acting ambassador in Mexico. At the same time he asked if it would be possible to have me assigned to a special commission that would enable me to work with him in the field of foreign affairs. The Minister's secretary brought the appointment to the Hilton that very evening. (The kindness of Fidel's manner that day and his taking the trouble to acquire the ambassadorship for me were the reasons why in October 1960, instead of resigning that post, I wrote to him asking him to fire me—to himself take back, in other words, what he had given me. Because if Fidel had forgotten the gentle memories of his friendships, I had not.)

I worked out of my room at the Hilton, and before many hours passed I saw that my room was too small to accommodate the great number of people I had to receive. The management offered me a suite in the east wing of the twentieth floor. Beautifully appointed, rimmed with a terrace, it had a drawing room with walls of glass, a large bedroom, and from just about everywhere an immense view of Havana, my Havana . . . the quay, the harbor, the city, the sea, the sky. That view began to restore the joy of living that I had lost in Mexico. In addition, I was given the use of the best automobile in the Ministry of Recovered Property compound—a new Cadillac which the mayor of Havana had received just before fleeing the country. It had every luxury, including a telephone and a two-way radio for communicating with the various branches of the government, particularly the army. I also had a chauffeur assigned to me, by Celia, but let him go after the first frantic day. Havana was full of wrecked automobiles lying discarded and useless as a result of the wild driving of those bearded soldiers, and the one serving as my chauffeur was threatening to create another wreck. I decided, despite the official plates, to drive it myself.

One of the first jobs I was given by Fidel and Celia was to attend to an American who had once spent a month with them in the Sierra Maestra and subsequently made favorable reports via radio and newspaper. He had been invited to witness "Operation Truth," and was now waiting to tape an interview with Fidel to be broadcast by an American network. At the moment, Fidel had no time, but he did not want the American to feel neglected. I asked the telephone girls of the Hilton to connect me with him—he was staying at the Hilton, it turned out—and I told him that Fidel promised to hold the interview as soon as possible, and if in the meantime there was anything I could do, to please let me know. He replied that he would come to see me right away. Fifteen minutes later a young man appeared—about thirty, pleasing in appearance though somewhat ungainly, and with an extraordinarily gentle aspect, and a graceful, ingenuous modesty.

For two days he was with me almost constantly, helping me to receive people and to summarize articles printed in American periodicals, as well as with the writing of important letters in English. His excellent manners were an agreeable contrast to the primitive harshness of Fidel's milieu. He was glad to have something useful to do with his time, he said. In fact, he had introduced himself as a free-lance writer, and added, "That means I'm out of a job." "Operation Toys," in which Fidel and some others were to drop toys to the children in those areas of the Sierra Maestra that had been the targets of the napalm bombs, took place at that time. As my American friend had already proved himself so useful in my office, I asked him to accompany ten foreign correspondents in my stead.

162

His return from "Operation Toys" three days later (everything was called an "operation" in that post-war year, even carnivals) was preceded by a big bouquet of flowers which was added to those that already filled my drawing room from end to end. (Oh, the times of plenty!) That night, for the first time in years, I wore evening clothes and went dancing. The following evening he took me to a movie. What follows is familiar to anyone who has ever had an idyl. He returned to the United States with his taped interview, came back in a fortnight, and again in a month. He would call me from New York two or three times a week. Then, on St. Valentine's Day he appeared in my doorway with a bouquet of red roses and the question: "Will you be my valentine?"

But if the personal side of my life was progressing in a most pleasant fashion the same could not be said for the official side. True, my position of responsibility (my friends jokingly called me "Fidel's Foreign Minister") and my nearness to Fidel, who at the moment was God to the Cubans, meant that I had great influence. I had only to pick up one of my three phones to reach the President of the Republic or the Ministers or the military chiefs personally and have the matter settled on the spot. My personal passes opened all doors for the foreign newspapermen. But I was continually harassed and compromised in the performance of my work by Fidel's unpunctuality and exasperating unreliability.

To my office came not only journalists but any foreigners who wished to see Fidel: financiers, proponents of a World's Fair in Cuba, motion-picture and television producers wanting to film Castro's life, industrialists with projects for installing factories, artists eager to make portraits of him, or caricatures, or statues, actors and actresses, and authors, and personalities from all over. It was as if the signal had also been given for audacious adventurers of every stripe to invade Cuba with fabulous projects, all based on the provision that we finance them.

Exiles from the various countries of Latin America arrived at my door seeking support for their causes. One expedition did leave for Nicaragua from Cuba, but was unsuccessful. (Later, when Fidel's inexplicable and unpredictable changeableness was in full swing, he seemed to forget the treatment he had received and deplored in Mexico and had many of the exiles arrested, accusing them of wanting to involve Cuba in conflicts, and of being motivated by the U.S. State Department.) One of the more redoubtable "invasions" that assaulted me consisted of the representatives of public-relations agencies in the United States. Those persistent people pursued me even up to—and on several occasions *into*—the hotel's swimming pool, when I would manage to get away for a swim on an odd Sunday. Once they trapped me, they displayed voluminous portfolios of documents and projects, along with their plans for "managing Castro."

Manage Castro! They were speaking of a man who not only was not manageable by others, but was incapable of managing himself. With growing despair I observed the truth of the saying that no one can govern others who cannot govern himself. Day by day I saw how Fidel, lost in the labyrinth of power, tangled everything by his clumsiness, then in desperation sought clattering solutions. Fidel is a man of action, not of thought and reflection. Martí once wrote: "Foresight is the essential quality in the constitution and government of peoples. Governing is no more than the act of foreseeing. The country must be saved from the open animosity or the greedy friendship of the other nations." Fidel, alas, had no foresight. He was always local in his conception of things. His mind, unlike his name, could not spread out internationally. Because his ego enveloped and confounded him, he could only see things in terms of the immediate; he could detect what was nearby, but could not look ahead, and therefore was pathetically unqualified to be a ruler. By his nature he was unable to stop and consider and to look about him. His obsession to excel forced him into extravagance, into destroying all that was established and organized. I could see these things at close quarters in Havana, just as the world later saw them in the way he rushed into the expropriation of whatever was left to expropriate, all at one blow—something no Communist revolution had done—on his return to Cuba from the United Nations in October 1960. He seemed to be doing it out of sheer spite; and he did not stop there, but proceeded to convert Cuba into a Russian dependency, drenched with Communist slogans in both Spanish and Russian, permeated with the Soviet ideology, bristling with Soviet-bloc weapons; he even went so far as to forcibly destroy the Cuban family as a social organism.

When I started working with Fidel I tried, by setting the example, to spread around myself an atmosphere of normalcy and dignity and efficiency. But he and those who surrounded him continued to live as if they were still in the Sierra Maestra, and nobody could get them down from there. My only possible ally was Captain Yanes, but Yanes was himself the principal target for the hostility of Fidel's associates, particularly of Celia. Celia managed the guard, which felt even closer to her than to Fidel himself, and all its members waged open warfare against Yanes. In our endeavor to establish a semblance of order, we two were sadly outnumbered.

Fidel's associates must have known—more through instinct than premeditation—that if Fidel were to change, if he were to shave and dress like any normal government figure, install himself in an office and study the nation's problems with care, surround himself with capable advisers, receive people in an orderly way and set up consultations with experts on each problem and project, there would no longer be a place for them in his existence. And so they all worked to prevent Fidel from organizing and normalizing his life. With his own proclivity for disorder, and his evident maladjustment after having left behind the freedom of the mountains, Fidel was more like a caged buffalo than a government figure; and it was so much easier for them to follow the current than to oppose it. The night our American friend finally made his taped interview—at four o'clock in the morning—the last question was: "How did you feel after you came down from the mountains?" Then Fidel's fatigue seemed to lie heavily on him, his look went suddenly far away, he was back in the forest, in the clear mountain air. "I miss my mountains," he replied softly—while on the other side of the door an excited crowd shoved and elbowed to devour him with more problems, more petitions. He rose absently to leave the room, and all at once I gave him, for the first and only time in my life, a kiss on his bearded and probably unwashed cheek. I felt at that moment an overwhelming tenderness for that poor creature who was often no more than a big child lost in a jungle of human problems and conflicts. I could not then think, nor could I ever have imagined, that this anguished man would one day in his conscienceless desperation go to the extreme of ordering the execution of his own companions, and bring so much affliction to Cuba.

At the beginning of February, Fidel, up to then Commander in Chief of the Armed Forces, became Premier. This was an inevitable step, because, as he himself said, the government did nothing. It did nothing because it had no authority. Despite Fidel's insistence that people go to the constituted government authorities with their problems and projects, it was to him that they came, because it was widely known that even President Urrutia and his cabinet ministers did nothing without first consulting the man who had given them their posts and who was the acclaimed idol of the entire population. In order to protect the norms of civil legality, Dr. José Miró Cardona cleared the way by submitting his resignation, and himself suggested that Fidel be called upon to occupy the position of Premier. Fidel was not at all happy about it. In my presence he reminded Celia that it was she who had insisted on his accepting the post. He went through with it, but unwillingly, for it brought more responsibility and restricted even further his cherished sense of personal freedom.

We were now able, in our work, to count on the assistance of his new offices, in addition to the Ministry of Foreign Affairs, to help us attend to diplomats and other visitors of special importance. But things continued to be chaotic. My position with respect to Fidel's guard, that "aristocracy of the Sierra Maestra," was as unstable as was Yanes's until matters came to a head one day when those mountaineers tried to prevent my entering Fidel's suite. I was with a U.S. Congressman and our lawyer in the United States, Constantin Kangles, who had an appointment. Fidel was sleeping, and Celia was out. The guards stopped us in the hall, and one of them paraded his authority, pointing out that he had "fired many bullets in the *sierra* and would not mind firing a few more." I grew angry and reminded him and his whole bunch once and for all that if they had fired many bullets in the mountains I had worked hard in Mexico to make that firing possible. And I started toward Fidel's suite despite his warning that he would fire and went inside and woke Fidel against the violent resistance of his personal escort. From that day on I had some authority over the mountain veterans. Fidel gave an order that wherever he might be, I was never to be prevented from reaching him.

Other incidents did not end on so agreeable a note. Mr. John Aaron literally almost died of apoplexy in the process of producing the "live" Person-to-Person program in which Fidel appeared with his son, Fidelito. It had been agreed that Fidel would give a few minutes of his time some days before the show to arrange camera placements, the questions that might be asked, and so on. But five days before the program was to go on, Fidel went off to the Sierra Maestra. I was used to tranquilizing those who had to wait for Fidel, but as the days went by and Fidel did not reappear, Mr. Aaron began to suffer more and more, and finally just sat looking at the wall while I sent messages to Fidel, via airplanes of the Rebel Air Force and by official and commercial radio, reminding him of his appointment. I was certain that he would show up as he had promised, for the Fidel I knew at that time always kept his word. It was one of his proudest claims. (It is surely a cause of despair to him that, unable to make good his wild promises, he can no longer honestly make the boasts on which his arrogance once fed.)

Fidel arrived twenty minutes before the show was due to start. It had been planned for him to be presented in "domestic relaxation," and a whole wardrobe of civilian clothes had been made ready; but none of the suits was large enough, and Fidel had none of his own. Recourse was had to a pair of pajamas, and the disconsolate Mr. Aaron produced a fine dressing gown to wear over them. He seemed prepared for all eventualities—but not the eventuality named Fidel Castro. The rage he flew into when he saw that dressing gown (it was too luxurious for him) was of epic quality. With seven minutes left, Fidel, who had not slept for two days, suddenly shut himself up in a room and furiously threw himself on the bed. Even Celia did not dare go in and speak to him. I went in, closed the door, and sat on the edge of the bed. I talked to him softly but firmly, as one talks to an obstinate child. He was lying face down, in a perfect rage, his head buried in pillows. The few moments of rest he had while lying down helped him to return to his senses, but he refused to wear that dressing gown, which, it is true, suited neither his personality nor his office. He would wear pajamas—but not the ones he had on. We called Yanes, who ran up to get Fidel's own striped ones, but was not in time. With one minute to go I had to impose a condition upon Aaron, that Fidel be shown only from the waist up.

As soon as he came under the lights, the "dragon" grew tame. He was another person. What a great actor was lost to the stage! When he wished, this Cuban Jekyll and Hyde could be captivating.

He had another tantrum one morning while Celia was raging against Yanes. It was the only time I ever saw Celia in such a state. She had made a list of those whom Fidel was to receive, but Yanes had been given the same assignment, and on this particular morning two groups of people came together with appointments for the same times. Yanes bore up under her attack like a perfect gentleman and with a bearing that contrasted significantly with the lack of control of the rebel "aristocracy." The whole thing was so unpleasant and depressing that suddenly Fidel started emitting frightful yells, clutched his head, and threw himself face down upon the bed in an absolute loss of self-control. Using the strongest possible language, he screamed hysterically that he be left alone, and kicked furiously. With a deep sense of discouragement and pain, I realized that it had fallen to me to be nursemaid of an uncontrolled, uncontrollable child. But there was no alternative. He was a symbol, and my friend, and had to be helped.

I led the two disputants away from him and put them into another room, begging them to come to an agreement and co-ordinate their assistance to Fidel, for the good of Fidel and of our collective task. Then I leaned on the balcony railing and gazed dismally out over the harbor. Below me the crowd clamored for that uncontrollable young man who was kicking his feet on a bed like a hysterical child—while outside, his image expanded, making of him a local god and an international apostle. Power, like revolutions, I thought, devours its children. I began to understand the tragedy of Cuba. For the first time I asked myself if, in order to herd the masses into a state of adoration and to become the supreme leader of a revolution, it is not necessary, as an indispensable prerequisite, to be mentally unbalanced.

chapter

12

One day the sister of Antonio Guiteras (Grau's Secretary of the Interior in his first administration, who was assassinated by Batista) wished to see Fidel. She had two of her friends bring me a letter for him. Fidel refused even to accept the letter, which I considered it my duty to get him to read. He stood looking at me for a moment, then said quietly, "She was living in Mexico when we were there, was she not?" I nodded. "She was there when you came to visit us in jail, was she not?" I nodded again. "And yet," he said, "we never saw her." He kept looking at me, then said gently, "Do whatever you like with the letter," and he left the room.

I remember the incident particularly well because it was, I think, the only time he ever looked at me and spoke to me with real affection in all the time I worked with him in Cuba. It was the only reappearance of the Fidel I had known in Mexico. Except for those few moments, the metamorphosis into a kind of dehumanized Savonarola clamoring for the end in Cuba of all that signified normalcy continued. In all the time I was there he never went to a motion picture or listened to music on the radio or watched television—except to listen to the speech of a possible opponent. As soon as he was satisfied that the speaker was not voicing opposition, he lost interest in the speech. He never read a book; nor did I ever see one in his immediate vicinity. Documents he merely skimmed over.

In the newspapers he read only what was said about him. I never heard him joke. As for women, he entertained them sometimes, tolerating them because they pursued him. His one true mistress was the revolution.

Just as he never seemed to long for Lilia, not once in all that time did he ever so much as mention the name of Cándido, or evoke that bygone period. I do not know if the memory of our dead friend afflicted him with remorse, or if Cándido no longer mattered because he was no longer useful to him. At times Fidel would look at me with a surge of sympathy and affection; at other times I would feel him staring fixedly at me with actual hostility. Of what did I remind him—I, a silent witness of the time when he was not yet the great Fidel Castro? I never learned his thoughts. He tried to be fair, giving me the ambassadorial post, and kept me working beside him (of course, he knew I was loyal and useful to him). But we never again had the kind of personal, human conversation we had often had in the past—a past buried under dreams, dead friends, and ingenuous, truncated romances. Possibly he realized that he could never impress me or make me see him as the others now did. Though I think he knew I was very fond of him, I also think he was aware that I always looked upon him as an adult looks upon an outstanding child—outstanding, but, still, a child. This was not the sort of reaction he was used to. Apart from those of his constant circle, the response to the mere sight of him was loud and physical. Wherever he went, people crowded around him deliriously, touching him as if he were a talisman, all speaking at once, hammering him with petitions, reminders, letters, filling his pockets with scraps of paper, shouting to be heard over the rest.

Sometimes, feeling suddenly fed up with his urban confinement in a hotel suite, he would jump up and cry "Let's go" to his escort, and start for the elevator while the sol-

172

diers grabbed their guns and followed him. Frowning, with that sullen, stubborn expression that had come to identify him and that gave him the appearance of being very angry, he would stride to his automobile, chauffeured by a mountaineer who drove like a madman, and disappear for many hours. Sometimes he went to La Cabaña Fortress to watch target practice, sometimes to Camp Liberty (formerly Columbia). Or he made unexpected calls to some government bureau or other, or to a girl-friend. Or occasionally he would simply go walking along the water-front promenade, the Malecón. Immediately a howling procession boiled up and turned his little walk into a demonstration. He could not do any of the simple, normal things people do. When he went off secretly to see a girl, all Cuba knew and talked about it, and wondered if she was going to be Fidel's new wife. He lived in an enormous goldfish bowl. But that is one of the horrors of power. It was the price that life was making him pay for desiring to be the factotum in everything. Admittedly, considering his enormous popularity, it would not have been an easy thing for him to avoid, but it might have helped matters if he had refrained from impetuously overriding the decisions of the authorities whenever it pleased him to do so.

Seeing him besieged like that, I, who on a lesser scale had just gone through the same thing in the embassy in Mexico, knew what he had to feel as he stood at the center of a perpetual whirlwind of hands wanting to be shaken or only to touch him. One ends by feeling every touch as if it were a jolt of electricity. The most sane and normal person must finally evolve into a temperamental, hysterical "prima donna" and want to smash something, feel ready to burst, feel that his patience is gone and that he can no longer give his attention to anyone at all. In Fidel's case it was a whole country that was spilling over him.

There was, of course, a way to prevent this. That way

173

consisted, quite simply, of not squandering himself (he had, after all, an escort to protect him); of not delivering himself up physically to the multitude in that orgy of demand and bestowal. But this was precisely what he lent himself to with most gusto. He enjoyed being acclaimed and sought after. He liked receiving approval, applause, adoration.

There was a great deal of sexual urgency in the way the women acclaimed him (and also some types of men). It was a time of virility-consciousness, which swelled into something that could not be checked. The only thing that mattered was to wear a beard and carry a gun. In the store where I bought my dresses the employees in sudden transports caught hold of my arm or hand, saying, "Oh, let me touch you—you are close to *him!*" When Fidel detached himself from an adoring crowd and jumped into his automobile he would be frowning, and his eyes, on the ride back, would be swimming as if he were drunk. His exhaustion would usually be the greater for his having gone without sleep for long periods of time. Meanwhile the irritability to which he was prone attacked him more frequently as his ability to control it grew weaker.

It is not true, as has been claimed, that he used drugs in order to go without sleep. Working ceaselessly was one of his ways of imposing the image of himself as a superman. Apparently he felt that this gave him a greater authority. He always—even in Mexico—liked to appear busy. But his endless comings and goings, after the victory at least, were largely a misuse of time. I found this out, not only from working with him, but from the times I had to go tracking him down when he was needed unexpectedly.

The misuse of time was particularly vexing to me, for it left me with little opportunity to transact official business. I had to wait hours to talk to him, and then there were constant interruptions. I never had enough

174

time to get through the pile of pressing problems I had brought that needed his authorization. Often I found him so distracted by the enveloping press of people, with his eyes dancing in that intoxicated way, that I went away again. It would have been like talking to a cataract. With so much to do and no opportunity to do it, I had to remember that song which ends: ". . . If I must die of thirst beside the fountain . . ." Of what use was I to anybody there? This was the feeling that was beginning slowly to unfold within me even as I spent hours exploring ways in which I might be useful and constructive.

Being a woman brought me a few unlooked-for problems. I remember a morning when I was awakened by a loud knocking on my door. I opened it in surprise, and in came Celia like a bullet, asking, "Isn't Fidel here?"

"Here?" I said. "Certainly not."

Seeing that the second bed in my bedroom had not been slept in, she swept on with insane haste to the drawing room, then left without further explanation, followed by the official escort which had waited outside. I understood then that I would have to reassure her completely so that she would not again fall victim to stupid confusions of that nature. Though it was comical, I was not amused by her insinuation. I was not amused because it meant that in my official work with Fidel I must thereafter go to extra pains to leave no room for doubt or suspicion, and outside of that work have as little to do with him as possible. What was comical was the fact that such a thought had never entered my mind, nor, I am sure, had it ever entered Fidel's. It was simply not the nature of our relationship, nor ever had been. In Mexico, of course, any attractive lady who happened to pass near Fidel received a long look as he turned his head all the way around to follow her with his eyes. But that reflex too had been left behind in Mexico, along with so many other of his human qualities, and Cándido, and Lilia, and the rest of it.

It seems opportune, at this point, to say that Fidel's relationships with his women seem always to have been as restless as his political life. We have seen his mother's indifference toward him. Her attitude did not change after the victory. Never did I see her come to visit Fidel. The first Mother's Day she had a chance to spend with all her children was in 1959, and she happened to be in Havana. She went off instead to her house in Oriente Province, to spend it with her own mother. On other levels he was equally unfortunate. His wife, Mirta, came from a thoroughly *batistiana* family; her brother, in fact, was a minister in Batista's cabinet. Fidel was divorced from her while he was in the Isle of Pines Penitentiary—although they appeared to love each other—because a government payroll published by a Batista politician listed his wife's name in a post in which she did not work, but for which she received a salary. They had a lovely boy, Fidelito, whose custody he gave to Mirta. While Fidel was in Mexico, Mirta remarried, and it was at that point that he proposed to Lilia. When he was thinking of leaving Mexico on the *Gramma* expedition, he sent for the boy, to avoid his being taken as a hostage by the Batista people. Mirta let him go, with legal authorization and in the care of Lydia, Fidel's half-sister, who loved the boy very much. But when Fidel was in the Sierra Maestra, Mirta came to Mexico and took the boy back to Cuba. (She had him kidnapped by some thugs from the automobile in which he was riding to Chapultepec Forest. We did not know who had done it, or that he was safe, until we learned that he was in the Cuban embassy with Mirta.) After Batista's fall, Fidelito returned to live with Lydia, in Cuba, but he missed his mother and his two little half-sisters (daughters of Mirta's second marriage), and Fidel let him go back to her.

176

There was another woman, who caused much comment in Cuba. She was married, and the affair began when she started writing him while he was on the Isle of Pines. Discovery of one of the letters almost caused the lady to be divorced. After the victory, when she was divorced, Fidel went about with her for a while, and it was rumored that they would marry. But they never married, and it seems he finally stopped seeing her.

We already know of Lilia. What Celia's precise relationship with Fidel was, I cannot say for sure. She was aware of all his little escapades with his admirers, none of which ever amounted to anything, and she generally knew whom he was with, and when. They never seemed to disturb her, at least on the surface. It is apparent, I think, that despite the inordinate and irrational scramble for Fidel's favors that took place following the victory, there was a lack of tenderness in his life (Celia came too late) that must have been profoundly damaging to a man of his sensitivity and pride. I think I sensed this the first time I met him; it was why I instantly conceived a tender, almost maternal affection for him.

*   *   *

While the country struggled to recover its equilibrium, Fidel got into a habit of talking to it via television. His "talkathons" ran on for five or six hours, easily breaking Chibás' record. He would keep Cuba's workers and functionaries before their TV sets until five in the morning. It disrupted the country's working rhythm, but Fidel did not think of that—and who would dare ask the workers and civil employees for an explanation when they were late to work the following morning? When those prodigious "talkathons" ended, Fidel would be in a zombie-like trance, his eyes unfocused, his thoughts devoid of congruity and coherence.

The loss of working hours on whatever pretext did not

disturb him in the least, as long as it was his doing. National work stoppages ranged in time from minutes to days. After the three-day "Victory Strike" that followed the fall of Batista, the "strikes" were resumed whenever it occurred to him to have a mass demonstration for some reason or other. He never waited for it to be a day of festivity or rest, but immediately ordered the suspension of all work. There were stoppages for the explosion of the ship *La Coubre,* for funerals, for celebrations, for the support of legislative measures. When he fired President Urrutia, he called for a fifteen-minute work stoppage in protest against the deposed Executive. He ordered one of several hours as a protest against the "counter-revolution" of Commander Hubert Matos—whose crime consisted of sending his friend, Fidel, a letter of resignation because of Fidel's move toward communism. That stoppage was accompanied by a huge rally—the one in which the sinister cry of *"paredón!"* ("to the wall!") was born. He never seemed to consider or to understand the fact that hundreds of thousands of pesos in production labor were being lost to the nation as a result of these senseless collapses. Some of those work stoppages took place while I was there. I never saw that they resulted in anything beneficial, except for the satisfaction they afforded Fidel, and the diversion they provided for the hundreds of truckloads of peasants who poured into the capital on a rare chance to see the city.

The highlight of all these occasions was a speech by Fidel. Sometimes, as at a rally, he made a personal appearance, sometimes it was only televised. But it was always long. The transitory and undulant nature of his emotional condition was reflected in those speeches. His oratorical manner oscillated between that of the patient and constructive logic of the teacher and the aggressiveness that is the backbone of his general behavior. He would harangue or cajole or rant or explain, as the occasion demanded. I noticed, moreover, that he became more aggressive by far when he was speaking in an open place than when he was under a roof. The intoxicating stimulus of crowds fed his aggressiveness to the bursting point. Between him and the crowd crackled a vicious current of hysterical irresponsibility that he used like Olympian thunderbolts to excoriate those who had offended him with an act of impiety.

Shortly after a somewhat mellowed old-time revolutionary named Paco Cairol published an article entitled "Let's Not Deify Fidel" (for which I congratulated him, to his surprise), the first blow fell on the freedom of the press. And the victim was none other than our old comrade Mario Llerena, whom Fidel had so often singled out for special assignments during the revolution. It was all over a simple, constructive warning, counseling Fidel to get himself organized now that he was the country's ruler. Fidel was furious. I tried to defend Llerena, but encountered a wall of stone; he refused to let me continue speaking when I mentioned Mario's name. He then went on television and dedicated a whole program to attacking Llerena with utmost irony. Needless to say, such an attack signified the sentence of proscription. I had Mario come to my suite at the Hilton and tried to make excuses for Fidel. What was the use? Llerena could no longer be published anywhere in Cuba.

Many were thus crucified by Fidel in his aggressive appearances on television. Without a single written law he thereby effectively suppressed the freedoms of thought and of press. On his weekly "Face the Press" programs no one dared ask questions that might have implied the slightest doubt of the young ruler's governing or legislative ability.

In his talkathons Fidel spoke continually of the fact that the revolution was financially limited, that we were poor, that we must be economical. Yet one of the peculiarities of the Castros in power was their penchant for chartering planes on what was often nothing more than the gratification of an irresponsible whim. Raúl, with a sizable retinue for company, made trips to Houston, to various countries in South America, to Czechoslovakia. His wife, Vilma Espín, went off to attend a Women's Congress in Chile, and to everyone's astonishment her delegation consisted of no less than eighty women—more than all the other delegations combined. And one day it occurred to her that she would like to make a trip to Czechoslovakia with some military friends of her husband's, while Raúl was there, and so off she went, in a special plane once again. Later, as you will see, there were giant expeditions to the United States, Canada, and Latin America when most of those who accompanied Fidel were merely along for the ride. All this, of course, was done with the public funds, while Fidel continued to belabor the population with tearful earnestness about how poor we were, and how we must do without comforts for the good of the country.

To dramatize his sincerity, Fidel moved from the Hilton to a house in Cojímar. The house was terribly uncomfortable for his guard, which lived in cramped quarters, was fed at irregular times or, on some days, not at all, and suffered nocturnal attacks by hugh mosquitos that drove one to despair. Having made his public display of thrift, Fidel rarely slept there after that first night, but it continued to be the headquarters of his guard. A room in Yanes's suite at the Hilton was set aside for him and he went there to sleep after his exhausting television speeches. Every time he made a constructive speech I gave him a "prize"—a rose which I left in a slender vase that stood in his room in Yanes's suite. The first time I left the flower, I put with it a little card of explanation. And he was so pleased whenever he found a flower there!— like a boy who has received a high grade. When he made

180

a destructive speech, on the other hand, my censure consisted of more than not leaving a rose; sometimes I would disappear for two or three days. And when he made his wild declarations announcing that he would destroy, ruin, hold executions (his constant threat in all troublesome situations), I would watch him fixedly and in silence. He would pause and listen to the cheers and *olés* of his cohorts in particular—it always reminded me of the blood lust of the bull fight—then his wandering look would rest on me for a moment and he would frown and give a muffled snort, like a bull, without deigning to articulate his thought in words.

The other members of his tight group lost no opportunity to represent my reproofs as those of a heretic. Nor did they ever forgive me for not joining the unconditional chorus of yeses and cheers, for not being afraid of him, for not diminishing myself in my dealings with him. They resented my willingness to risk infuriating him when it was a question of fairness, or of getting him to do something he ought to do. I cared enough about him to contradict him if it was necessary. If I refrained from becoming part of that Fidel-is-always-right sect it was because I knew that blind approval fed not his strength, but his weakness, his vulnerability. It was by never contradicting him that the Communists were eventually able to infiltrate the government and take power. By pricking him into extended activity, as one stimulates a bull to continue charging, heightening his aggressive tendencies, they were able finally to secure him firmly in a tangle without solution.

The fits of depression he is said to suffer nowadays are reflected in his television appearances—particularly in his language, full of persecution mania and key words that clearly indicate an abnormal state of mind. It is said that he has been under electric-shock treatment. (It is also widely known in Havana that the physician who attended him until recently, a Dr. Sorhegui, had studied "brainwashing" in Iron Curtain countries; and that when he died suddenly, of a heart attack, Raúl Castro appeared in his office and carried off his papers.)

One of the main problems of the M26–7 before the victory was how to acquire funds, but by the time Batista fell, the movement possessed a fund of $5 million. In addition to the donations received from abroad with increasing regularity, contributions were exacted from all the sugar-mill owners by the Revolutionary Government in the mountains, which established a Revolutionary National Treasury to receive the taxes which until then had gone to the Batista government. After the victory, Celia, along with her other duties, also handled this money, and in the most colorful way imaginable. Just as our grandfathers did with their savings, she kept the money in a small metal box on the floor of her room. It was not even a safe, but simply a small metal coffer with a handle on the lid. (During the two months she and Fidel were at the Hilton, for example, it was to her that the soldiers of the escort, the guard, and other units came for expense money.) Celia did not bother with receipts or accounts. She merely opened the money box, filled to the top with large bills, and doled it out generously. The first time I saw her do this I was astonished beyond measure. Rooms in the hotel were rent-free for the soldiers who lived there, by courtesy of the hotel. But meals had to be paid for. To eat at the Hilton, which was among the most expensive restaurants in Havana, it was necessary only to sign one's name. The "revolution" paid. Any rebel soldiers who wished could enjoy this remarkable privilege, whether they lived in the hotel or elsewhere. They brought along their relatives, friends, and girl-friends to visit the hotel from top to bottom, then treated them to a meal. It was not only the soldiers; great numbers of adventurers came from everywhere: pseudo-journalists, false "functionaries," and foreign women—some of an obvious professional group—settled at the Hilton (their rooms *did* have to be paid for) and came out of the hotel's stores with everything they could lay their hands on, including gold wrist watches, merely by signing their names. One lady in a single day ran up a bill of $52 in the beauty salon. I saw my friend Commander Pedro Miret pay a bill of $150,000 to the management for the soldiers' meals alone. Soon afterwards there was another payment of $100,000. And the bills kept coming.

When I mentioned it to Fidel, he ducked the issue. He did not want to hear a word about bills. Everyone else I tried to approach on the subject was always "very busy." The management, naturally, would do nothing without a direct order from Fidel. By taking unilateral action, and by paying for my meals every day to set the example, I finally managed to end the business of signing for meals and purchases. Even so, it took me almost two months to accomplish, for although the soldiers gradually followed my example, I still had to see to it that the others, particularly the adventurers, complied.

All money matters were a mess around Fidel. In addition to the Hilton "open house," there were the enormous bills that went unpaid: the M26–7 millions, of which no public accounting was ever made; the checks Fidel impulsively wrote out for fanciful projects; the forthcoming trip to the United States with its caravan of superfluous traveling companions. One day, I was told, Fidel wrote out a check for $100,000 for a man who came to him with a project for planting rice in the Zapata swamp—a project which ended in total failure. Another time he wrote a check for $300,000 against his account at the Postal Savings Box of the Ministry of Communications, putting the management in a quandary because, as it turned out, the check was not covered.

Since he had left the Hilton, my work had been made

more difficult by the fact that when it was necessary for me to be present I now had to go to Cojímar or to the presidential palace, or wherever the appointment was, to learn that he would be late, or had simply disappeared. At the beginning of March he left me high and dry with the second monthly press conference when he left the house at Cojímar five minutes before the arranged time. Our automobiles passed his at the entrance, and he did not even bother to stop.

One night there were fourteen people in my suite who had come from all parts of the world, and who had special, separate appointments with the Premier. Among them were Japanese correspondents from a mission that was visiting Cuba at the time, and an important German newspaperwoman. The Japanese and German embassies had officially solicited and obtained the promise of these interviews with Fidel, and the German woman was personally accompanied by her ambassador. The interviews were to be held at the presidential palace at eight o'clock.

As we were about to leave for the palace, Yanes telephoned to say that Fidel would not be able to see anyone before nine-thirty. Nine-thirty came and went and there was still no sign of Fidel. For entertaining people, the champion was my secretary, Isabel Bermúdez, and she outdid herself that evening. Isabel was an attractive, decent, well-dressed woman who was a friend of mine from the days of the university dramatic group. When I was officially installed at the Hilton, she had come to offer her services without pay. She did not need a job, but thought she would find that kind of work interesting. Miss "Bermyoudez" was thereafter an active participant in everything that took place in my office, and became very popular with the foreign newspapermen by virtue of her excellent humor in the bleakest moments, her talent for playing the accordion, and her ability to ease the ordeal of waiting by telling little jokes. She also knew

how to talk to Fidel with brisk sallies that left him momentarily tamed. In my suite, that evening, she played
the accordion delightfully as usual, and when we had run
out of excuses for Fidel, she said to the impatient visitors
with her charming smile, "You can't see Fidel, but on the
other hand you can see us, two very nice girls, and you
can hear me play the accordion." Annoyed as they were,
they began to laugh and the tension gave way to good
feeling and to songs and airs from all parts of the world.

At one o'clock I located Fidel, and got Celia on the
phone. She sounded amused and informed me that he
was busy with Che Guevara and under no circumstances
could he see anyone until later, and that I was to in-
vite them along to the Sugar Bar (the Hilton's roof garden) and "charge it to our account." Isabel went home,
and at three the others began to leave. After the German
ambassador and the Japanese journalists left, I escorted
the others to the Sugar Bar. By three-thirty Fidel could
no longer be located anywhere. I wore out my throat and
my imagination reciting Fidel's activities from the day
he was born, dramatizing his "thousands of very serious
preoccupations," trying like Scheherazade to make the
time pass unnoticed. The last one left at five.

In the "waiting for Fidel" competition, limited to
those with a fixed appointment, the easy winner was Mr.
Galloway, of the "U.S. News and World Report," who
waited a week. Frank Bartholomew, the president of
UPI, also waited a week, and finally left without seeing
him, but his appointment had not been definitely set.
Once I was approached by an American attaché with a
request for Fidel to receive fifty American newspaper editors. The appointment was for twelve at Cojímar. Fidel
arrived at three. The same treatment was accorded to the
economic commissions that were twice sent over from
England, and even to Herbert Matthews.

The day I brought Matthews and his wife to Cojímar

for their appointment with Fidel was one of my truly bitter experiences on that job. Something like it had already happened several times before, when the friends and collaborators of the Mexico days had come with great emotion to see him, in vain. And more than one of these good people had blamed me, whom they had asked to be their intermediary, and even renounced their friendship for me. How could I tell them what Fidel invariably said in answer to my insistence: "I'm very busy, I can't see them, tell them anything." The Matthews' appointment was for one o'clock in the afternoon. When Isabel and I arrived with them at Cojímar we found nobody there. Not even Celia. The only one I managed to roust out was the cook, Miguelito—the same fellow who had threatened to shoot me outside Fidel's suite that day at the Hilton. Miguelito, who was now a friend of mine, told me that "the Chief" had just left for La Cabaña fortress "to watch the soldiers on the firing range for a while." I used the telephone and the radio in my automobile, to no avail. Yanes came by and dashed out again to look for him. I felt so terrible that I could not force myself to return to the drawing room between efforts to trace Fidel, and I am certain that from that day on, Mrs. Matthews, whom I had met (and immediately liked) once before on a trip I had made to New York from Mexico in 1958, took a dislike to me for what she must have thought was my lack of consideration.

It was three o'clock when Señor Castro finally appeared, followed by Celia, who was loaded down with packages of food for his lunch. (His meals came from the best restaurants in Havana.) He looked into the drawing room and said hello and proceeded to the pantry, where I sat leaning on my elbows with my head in my hands trying to think of what to try next. With perfect serenity he waited for the food to be warmed up, then disposed of an enormous meal of magnificent preparations. He drew it out so long

186

that Isabel came and reminded him anxiously, "Fidel—Matthews is there."

"And I am here," was his reply, with so cynical and scornful an attitude that I fully understood how completely useless it was for anyone to expect him to remember past favors. I believe his overly proud nature considers any favor he has received to be a humiliation—and Fidel never forgets a humiliation. He had had to depend on Matthews and to feel indebted to him for the world's awareness and recognition of his revolutionary movement, and now he was getting his own back by making him wait. I was greatly relieved when, after he had finished eating, Fidel threw his arm around Matthews' shoulders and went off with him for a stroll through the gardens of that beautiful property, where they stayed for a long time talking.

When Fidel had come down from the Sierra Maestra, psychologists and psychiatrists had studied him with interest via his television speeches and public appearances, and the private diagnosis, as I afterwards learned from a professional psychologist who was a friend of mine, was paranoia. I myself have come to see Fidel as resembling several characters of Greek literature. When he plants himself like a man possessed, impelled by something inside him to kill, to destroy like a predestined exterminator, he is Orestes. When, like a crazed man, he rushes against non-existent enemy armies visible only to his warped mind, he is the tragic Ajax, the impressive and touching warrior blinded by the gods. But the one he most closely resembles in his best moments is Odysseus, with all his sly tricks, his daring, his valor, and his weaknesses. But Fidel has at least one weakness that Homer spared his hero: he wants to be a god, whereas Odysseus, when he had the opportunity to be one, had the greatness to prefer to go on being a man. It is this difference that as

187

a human being elevates Odysseus and condemns Fidel Castro.

One thing is certain: Fidel lives in tremendous tension. He is a wreckage of conflicts and contradictions. It is not for nothing that his first speech, in the hour of victory, was haunted with references to death, and that Cuba has been soaked with the tragedy-laden slogan: *"patria o muerte"* ("fatherland or death").

chapter

13

For all his resolute will, his tremendous faith, and his faculty to register the immediate circumstance, Fidel seemed to have a presentiment that his true gift was what superstitious people call "a lucky star." Except for the Moncada disaster, his most absurd and hasty undertakings kept turning out well. But that was when he was waging war against a hated tyrant. War is noise and peace is quiet, and what does Fidel do in time of quiet? He makes noise. What I do not believe (for reason will regain its eternal force at the expense of the "lucky stars") is that exceptional luck will continue very long with the one it has favored unless it is combined with order, care, and foresight. I think Fidel knows this. I think he knows that things have been coming to him as if fallen from the sky, that he does not deserve them, and that they will not last too long. He knows he must exploit that "star" before it fades.

One of the things Fidel applied his well-known haste to was the making of laws. The record was what mattered to him. In his first year a thousand laws were passed in the Council of Ministers. In all his laws and regulations it was easy to see that he was improvising, following his impulses of the moment. He would become enthusiastic over the wildest projects and order them to be started immediately, without the slightest concern for the administrative steps and financial responsibilities involved, and without troubling to get even elementary technical counsel. The many millions raised for the agrarian reform operations, like those five million the M26-7 had brought down from the mountains, were never accounted for. At the end of the "Year of Agrarian Reform" Cuba had to admit that during that time she had been forced to import 100,000 more tons of rice than in previous years.

Agrarian reform was one of the principal goals of the revolution. We were all agreed that through such reform we would help the poorest people on the island, as well as take a big step toward the stabilization of the economy. Unquestionably Fidel started out with good intentions. In his two years in the mountains he had come in close contact with, and been greatly affected by, the condition of the peasants.

Cuba's peasant population is estimated at 43 per cent. It is the part that suffers most and with greatest immediacy the periodic unemployment that comes every year with the long "dead season." It is the class that has always been undernourished and vulnerable to tuberculosis, intestinal parasites, and all the other illnesses born of poverty. These people live in the worst hygienic conditions. Their houses are thatched huts and hovels, whose walls, made of strips of palm bark, are easily carried off by the cyclones. The roofs are of palm branches, the floors are of earth, and in terms of comfort they are indistinguishable from the pigpens which are exactly the same except smaller. Very few of these peasant huts have electricity or bathrooms or running water. The water is drawn in buckets from wells and rivers, or is caught in rain barrels, where all species of parasites readily accumulate. More than 54 per cent of the peasant dwellings of Cuba lack sanitary service of any kind. The peasant has never enjoyed any medical service whatsoever, nor has he ever received adequate sanitary education.

The revolution's program of helping the peasant was therefore very dear to us all. When Fidel Castro came down from the Sierra Maestra after having seen with his own eyes the poverty and backwardness of these people, he was obsessed with helping and protecting them and was ready to take the most radical steps to do so. Projects were got under way to better their conditions; the construction of modern, hygienic dwellings in urban and rural areas was actually begun. It was not long, however, before the program bogged down for lack of funds and foresight, for reasons we shall presently come to.

In addition to houses for workers and peasants, the government also set out to build schools. The number built has not been as many as government propaganda claims, but in any event, as part of the construction program, this too was unable to continue, for lack of funds. Castro propaganda has gone so far as to claim that no schools had been built in the past fifty years, which is not true: even the Grau government put up educational centers, and also constructed a workers' quarter in Havana. Naturally many more are needed, but the present government has been unable to satisfy the popular need, as it had promised. When it came to power, there were five thousand graduate teachers out of work, while a considerable portion of the population was unable to acquire elementary education.

According to the official census of 1953, 31 per cent of Cuba's children of school age received no schooling whatever, and another 29 per cent had attended school three years or less. In many large rural areas, either there were no schools at all or they were so rare that to attend them the underfed, barefoot children had to travel great distances. Boys who did manage to attend school soon stopped going, as they were needed by their fathers to help with the work. It was the same in the cities, where the boys of the poorer classes left elementary school before completing all the grades. To remedy this situation, the Castro regime passed the Educational Reform Law, but was confronted by a shortage of teachers. What had become of those five thousand graduate teachers who should have been available? The answer is that the conditions imposed upon the teachers were unacceptable. And so the government has decided to use junior high school students in their place. As instruction in languages, music, and arts and crafts had been abolished, the teachers of these subjects were transferred to classes of general education, despite the fact that they did not have the necessary preparation.

What were those unacceptable conditions? Among other things, extra hours for teachers, who not only received no compensation but actually had their salaries lowered; militarization of children and adolescents, who are, moreover, given obligatory indoctrination in Communist ideology; suppression of several universities and all normal schools; and the refusal to establish the rural normals that are so indispensable for preparing a workable educational program for the peasantry. Those universities that are permitted to remain functioning are submitted to the dictates of the present policy. The autonomy of the University of Havana has been undermined through pressure applied by a committee director who owes his office to a few student-militia chiefs. Mass resignations by the professors who cannot accept these impositions are responsible for the fact that in the University of Havana, for example, many of the faculties are inactivated because of the scarcity of professors. A university professor, after all, cannot be replaced by a politician whose only qualification is that he is friendly to the regime.

The Educational Reform Law disdains the whole body of investigation and research that was carried out in the field of psychology and pedagogy in the last thirty years.

It is full of technical absurdities which it would take too long to analyze here. One of its "revolutionary" measures, incidentally, was to do away with the kindergartens, because they were "a privilege of the wealthy class." Instead of making them available to *all* the children, the leveling process was undertaken from the negative side, in keeping with the typical behavior of the present regime.

The whole intellectual and professional class of Cuba is opposed to the Castro dictatorship. Is it that all these and the entire middle class are capitalists, imperialists, reactionaries? Certainly not. *But they are the thinking class.* The spirit of Castroism echoes the same cry that a Spanish Falangist general hurled at the thinkers in his country during the Spanish Civil War: "Death to Intelligence!"

The program to build houses and schools was undermined, as I have said, by a lack of funds. This situation was brought about by a chain of laws that was passed, with each intended to counteract the errors of the preceding ones. In the end, little was achieved by all this legislative activity, and each law sowed a little more of the instability that finally paralyzed the economic life of the country. The Cuban building industry had been very strong before the victory, and its growth had been accompanied by a correspondingly rapid growth of the island's cities. Then it fell into a sluggish state in the post-revolutionary uncertainty. With regard to construction, Castro put through two laws. The first was the Rent Reduction Law, which imposed rent reductions of up to 50 per cent on all houses in Cuba. As a result, construction fell off alarmingly. The Urban Reform Law, which succeeded it was intended to establish a flat top rate of four dollars per yard of urban property regardless of location. The building industry, instead of gaining incentive from the second law, was paralyzed by it, and the result was profound economic insecurity. As a consequence, the harm done to the people through unemployment was greater than the widely proclaimed benefits derived from the reductions in rent and in the price of property. Continuing its effort to provide housing, the government tried to raise funds by creating the INAV (National Institute for Savings and Housing) to replace the old National Lottery, which in the past had brought a lush revenue to the politicians. Numbered bonds were substituted for the lottery tickets, but the people lost interest when the prizes were reduced, and they stopped buying the bonds. As a result, the funds so vitally needed for construction became virtually non-existent, and we were right back where we had started from.

One day I arrived at Cojímar to find Fidel in excellent humor and in the middle of a building project. He was walking up and down like an animal in a zoo and talking into the phone to Pastorita, a colorful woman who had been with the rebels in the Sierra Maestra and whom he had appointed head of the INAV. He pressed her to start in immediately to build houses, and while he strolled the length of the rooms with obvious enjoyment, he kept adding details of the most puerile kind, complete with gaudy color suggestions (pink kitchens, yellow dining rooms, etc.) for the various rooms—and all this without troubling to ask anyone for technical or financial advice. I watched in stupefaction as he raised a whole city in his imagination. It was an excellent proposal, and brought him great popularity, but the actual completion of most of those housing projects never went further than his imagination.

And yet Fidel, at the beginning, had the whole people at his disposition to try to help Cuban reorganization and reconstruction. He had the most capable technicians and professionals in all fields. He had excellent government ministers and functionaries, who were willing to believe that the early dislocation and confusion were due only

194

to growing pains, to the reconstruction of the economy, the hasty apprenticeship of a government that wanted to do the most possible good in the shortest possible time. But the young Premier never really wanted to surround himself with those who might have been able to teach him something. The best ministers and functionaries were made to feel uncomfortable and ended by leaving the government. The only possible explanation for Fidel's behavior is that he is primarily a politician and agitator, when what is needed in a Chief Executive is a statesman and administrator.

One of the excellent offers that passed through my office was of a spontaneous and anonymous "brain trust." A group of professors, technicians, and experts offered to send Fidel their information and opinions on the various national problems, and because they did not want him to suspect them of being interested in power or publicity they withheld their names. The first study was on agrarian reform, and was delivered to me personally. I was never able to get Fidel to read it. He was always "very busy"—too busy even to find out what was in it.

The whole of Cuba contributed to agrarian reform. It became the fashion to donate agricultural equipment and tractors. One talked of nothing else. The private schools competed with each other in trying to present a tractor. Girls of so-called "high society" stopped being frivolous and made collections for the farmers. The Association of Sugar Mill Owners even made a special collection and raised a million dollars for agrarian reform. (Fidel returned it to them in a fit of arrogance.)

Such contributions, from all over the island, make it clear that whoever says the people turned against Fidel only because he was threatening their interests is misrepresenting the facts. When Fidel took his first step that hurt the landlords, with the Rent Reduction Law, the landlords ended by agreeing that it was a just law, and accepted it. There was no thought of conspiracy, much less of counter-revolutions. I have heard more than one rich man in my country say, "If it is for the good of Cuba that my intake is reduced, no matter." A sugar mill owner who had given us $750,000 for the revolution once said to me, "God gave me so much that if they take a lot of it from me, I don't complain."

It is of course true that there was poverty in the cities and among the farmers. There was a great deal of it, as I think I have already made clear, particularly in the agricultural areas. But it was not all as my companions were painting it; nor to remedy the situation, was it necessary to destroy Cuba, as they have done. The cause of the farmers' poverty in our country is fundamentally not rooted in the large estates, but in the fact that they rely exclusively on the sugar industry, with its ups and downs and brief season of activity.

With regard to our large land-holdings, there is a demagoguery involved which derived from ignorance and was converted into a political weapon. From 1937 and as a consequence of the demands made by the revolutionary generation he had just defeated, Batista saw that if he was to consolidate his position he would have to find some sort of popular backing. Among his measures for social improvement, one was to include, within the Law of Sugar Coordination, the Right of Permanence, favoring those peasants who produced 375 tons of sugar cane annually per *caballería* (thirty-three acres), which on our soil in not difficult to accomplish. From 1937 on, no sugar-cane grower could be removed from the land he cultivated if he filled that quota, and as long as he paid a rent of 5 per cent of the annual product of that land. Also during that period the Minister of Agriculture, engineer Amadeo López Castro—who it seems was a man who protected and defended the farmers—extended property titles to the peasants who occupied lands that

196

went under the name of *realengos* (in colonial times such lands belonged to the King of Spain). These *realengos* were an old sore spot in the Republic, because many of them were American-owned.

In 1950, during Carlos Prío's presidency, the protection of the sugar-cane grower was broadened with a law that stated *that the grower would be required to pay no rent whatever for land on which he planted sugar cane, nor for an additional area necessary for crop rotation.* For the rest of the land he occupied (for cattle and other crops) he paid $15 annually for every *caballería* (forty-five cents per acre), without any limit on the amount of land he might occupy, provided that he filled the sugar-cane quota. As long as the grower kept that part of the bargain, he kept his rights.

In 1954, with Batista again in power and trying as in 1937 to win popular support; and in view, also, of the advanced workers' and farmers' legislation introduced in the years preceding his second dictatorship, he put through a law broadening still further the Farmer's Right of Permanence: anyone already occupying five *caballerías* (165 acres) or less had the Right of Permanence, even if he was a squatter—that is to say, even if he had settled on the land without a deed or a title and had begun to cultivate it.

The classic and dramatic dispossessions of farmers prior to 1937 were completely eliminated from rural Cuba from that year on. There were no more dispossessed sugar-cane growers, so that when Fidel Castro came to power the great private properties were more juridical properties than real ones. For example: the company named Atlántica del Golfo which owned 10,000 *caballerías,* only answered for, and had under cultivation, 300. The Tánamo Sugar Mill owned 3,000 and could cultivate only 100. (I cite these cases because I know them first-hand.)

In addition, the sugar-cane grower could sell his Right of Permanence at a price greater than the value of the land set down in the property registration, which at a distant beginning had been minimized by the owners so that they might pay less taxes; and after 1937, as they were unable to cultivate those lands and found themselves obliged to respect the Right of Permanence law, the value really was low because the individuals or companies who "owned" them did not own them in reality. The only right the owners had with respect to their uncultivated lands was to charge the top rent of 5 per cent of the value of the sugar cane produced on them (that is, until Prío's laws abolished the rents). This was one of the reasons why the Cuban landowners did not oppose or have reason to oppose agrarian reform. What they did complain about, once the Agrarian Reform Law was approved, was the anarchy involved in the calculation of future raw material; they could not be sure that the peasants would produce the minimum requirement of 375 tons of sugar cane per *caballería* annually. This anarchy emerged when the Castro government decided to abolish the Right of Permanence, thus eliminating the fixed production minimum, which finally harmed the government itself.

Fidel had all the sugar-cane lands (and others) placed in the hands of the INRA (National Institute of Agrarian Reform). With this reform bill, Cuba's 65,000 sugar-cane growers, 50,000 of whom had only two *caballerías* or less, found themselves with fewer rights than before.

INRA also lowered the daily wage of the cane cutters from $3.00 to $2.50, while increasing their hours from eight to nine, and suppressing Sunday pay. All this was "for the good of the working class."

It is for the good of the working class, then, that Cuba's State-controlled industries have become financially inoperable, that both the national income and the people's capacity to acquire goods have fallen off badly, that in the industries that have not closed down, their new employer (the state) lays off workers, lowers wages, lengthens workdays, pays in vouchers (as in the worst imperialistic times), and annuls all the gains won by the revolutionary struggles of the thirties.

Incredibly, what was not permitted the private employer must now be accepted from the State—"with enthusiasm and the spirit of sacrifice." Failure and lowered production is blamed on the *"yanquis."* Another of the complaints against "the Yankee octopus" was that it bought our sugar raw. Yet our new customer, Russia, not only buys it raw, but buys far less, and pays less for it. Thus, our *enfant terrible,* who began by ruining tourism and construction, and finished by ruining all the industries established in Cuba—all in the name of progress—has even managed to ruin Cuba's sugar industry. He boasted that we could do without the United States sugar quota. Then when the United States was pestered into removing the quota, which was what Castro had obviously wanted, cries of "victim" and "Yankee economic aggression" were heard. Then Fidel announced that we would sell our sugar to Russia. What Russia did not buy, he said, would be sold on the world market at a better price, because the United States would have to buy it there. (He likes to manufacture his own economic theories.)

Here is the reality and the result: Russia promised to buy, *for internal consumption,* five million tons in five years. (In 1958 the United States purchased, in that one year, a little over five million tons.) In 1960 Russia added another 700,000 tons to the million already contracted for. Of that 1,700,000 only 200,000 tons are payable in money—in dollars. The rest, one and a half million tons, is paid in trade. Russia pays about two cents less per pound than what the United States paid. It is estimated that the change of customers costs Cuba $165 million on every three million tons. Meanwhile, sugars offered by other countries of the Soviet bloc have begun to appear on the world market. This "mysterious" sugar, which undoubtedly is ours, has lowered the price on the world market of Cuban sugar left unsold. In other words, the marketing of our own product by the Soviet-bloc countries lowers the price of the remainder of Cuba's sugar, which is easily the greater part of her annual output. (In 1960 she produced over five million tons.)

Fidel unloaded the blame for his failures on landowners, landlords, employers, and his favorite target, the Americans, fomenting hatred in order to maintain a high spirit among the people and make them accept whatever he might say or command. But then all of Cuba began to see through the "advantages" it was supposed to have gained with its good faith, its support of Fidel, and its exchange of private employer for State employer. It answered with sabotage, with the gathering of insurgents in the mountains of Escambray, and the unprecedented exodus of whoever could manage to find a plane or a small boat. It was no longer only the rich and middle classes who fled. There were now workers and tenant farmers in exile. While the military tribunals and summary execution squads operated against revolutionists, police terror increased, the jails became packed with political prisoners, and concentration camps like that of Minas del Frío filled up day by day.

The lack of incentive caused crises in rural production, and resulted in a scarcity of things we formerly produced and now must import from the Soviet bloc. As for Fidel's favorite project, the Agrarian Reform Law, it was not even carried out. One reason for this is that the law, having been passed before the shift toward Communism, was not adaptable to Marxist tenets. It declared that the redistribution of land was to begin with government-owned land, proceed to wastelands, then move on to the large private holdings. But it was the last-mentioned that were pounced upon first, along with many small properties which were technically not subject to expropriation. In the latter case, a property needed only to be requested by some farmer to be snatched from its owner. The reason these lands were the first to be seized was that they were already cultivated. They were the easiest fields to work. Also they were useful to impress visitors from abroad. Such visitors saw beautiful harvests, roads, and irrigation works supposedly made by the revolution but which in fact were there before January 1959.

When the President of Indonesia, Sukarno, was invited to visit Cuba and was given the classic guided tour, he asked continually, "Did you make this?"

Invariably the reply was: "No, that was already here."

He saw co-operatives, schools, the Civic Plaza of Havana, highways, roads, and the question and its answer were almost always the same. They say that Che Guevara, who accompanied Sukarno, let slip an interjection, and said something in Spanish about how tiresome the man was being with his questions. President Sukarno turned to him and said in our language, "If you like, we can continue conversing in Spanish, señor Guevara." The fact is that the visit was cut short and that the government officials spoke very badly of him and of his "bad manners." From what I know, this Cuban revolution has never distinguished itself by its fine manners.

*　　*　　*

The contracts which the INRA confers under the Agrarian Reform Law are not title deeds of possession, for they are subject to the requisites of that law. Accordingly, the growers are prohibited from selling the property; from receiving official aid unless willing to enter a co-operative, and from transferring their ownership rights (in cases of inheritance) to more than one of the children. Naturally this last measure encourages bitter rivalry in the family, for the father must decide which one of his children will inherit all the rights to the land. It is even worse than the old primogeniture, and is another of the facets of that consanguinary war which Fidel has fostered in attacking the solid family formation of the Cuban people. It reflects his dissociation from his own, with which he has almost no relation at all, except for his brother, Raúl. I once even saw the guard insult one of his sisters (who had worked for the revolution) so brutally that the girl left the hotel in tears. Fidel also sent his family an order warning them not to seek government work, for fear that he be criticized.

Madame Lina Castro, however, has kept the Castro property intact. Close friends say she threatened to go into exile and create an international scandal. One of Fidel's sisters was less fortunate. He had her arrested and sent to the prison at La Cabaña because she had recommended certain contractors for a government project. This show of austerity on the part of Fidel hardly tallies with the irregularities and constant extravagance in which he himself lives. In his own words he lives "modestly," but the fact is he pays nothing, gets everything he desires, has several houses at his disposition, and is served the finest delicacies wherever he goes, while everyone finds himself at his service. He owns a Mercedes-Benz —which was not among the "recovered properties"—and that personal checkbook I mentioned earlier.

As time went by I became convinced that his secretiveness in Mexico with regard to his plans meant that, as in the Moncada attack earlier, he simply did not have concrete plans. Similarly, during the two years of the revolu-

202

tion the accusation was often heard that the M26–7 lacked a definite program. The movement was like a character in search of an author, looking for the program, the defined ideology which its founder was never able to furnish. Eventually, Mario Llerena, in Mexico, fashioned a program that momentarily rescued the movement from that accusation. It was an eminently conservative document; the furthest it went was to contemplate the possibility of nationalization of the public utilities. The document even negated the existence of imperialism. It was approved by Fidel Castro, and shortly afterwards Llerena was named chief representative of the M26–7 in exile. But the lack of a concrete ideology persisted within the movement. Nevertheless, an attempt is being made to credit Fidel with having drawn up a complete program of his aims as far back as 1953, at his trial after Moncada, when he defended himself with his "History will absolve me" speech. In this widely diffused document there would appear to be a complete plan of all that happened afterwards.

The fact is that what was published after the victory is not what Fidel Castro originally said at that private trial, as Manuel Urrutia, the deposed President of Cuba, knows. Urrutia, you will remember, was one of the magistrates; it was he who played so worthy a part on that occasion when Fidel wanted him to be Provisional President of Cuba during the revolution. He is, therefore, in a position to know that the document now being circulated has been altered to include statements which describe subsequent events, but which Fidel never made at the trial.

Jean Paul Sartre was with Fidel for a time in 1960, and although he was instinctively captivated (for who could be more existentialist than Fidel?), he said of the movement that it was "a revolution without method," and referred to the government officials as *"les enfants au pouvoir"* ("children in power"). What this means is that the boys who in Mexico had played "cowboys and Indians" are now playing "government" with the life and destiny of our country.

Little by little I began to see that my country's hopes for peace, after those cruel, bloody years of revolution, would not be achieved while Fidel Castro governed Cuba. Already, in April of that year, when we made our trip to the United States, there was beginning to be discontent among those who had been his companions and supporters. More than one came to see me and said, half jokingly, "Well, do we start conspiring?" Of course at that point the criticism was not yet serious, but for some time I had been noticing the grave injustices which the people were suffering. The deluge of complaints that came to me from outraged Cubans, including people who had been arbitrarily dispossessed of their land (before the passage of the Agrarian Reform Law), and even from rebels who had been unfairly treated, made me fearful at what I heard from the threatening lips of more than one: that soon Havana might witness a "St. Bartholomew's Night." I might turn up one fine morning hanging from a balcony of the Hilton, as Isabel jokingly told me. I would not abandon Fidel, but if something happened to me I wanted it known that I had not been blind, that I had seen the movement's awful mistakes, had lamented them, and had tried as much as I was able to dissuade the government from making them. Accordingly, before making the trip to the United States, I left a document with a friend, in which I told the truth about what was going on in those days, and asked her to make it public if anything happened to me.

As an illustration of the agrarian injustices that occurred even before passage of the Agrarian Reform Law,

204

one of the cases that appeared several times in my office was that of the granddaughter of General Calixto García. This woman owned a coffee plantation in the Sierra Maestra, where she lived with her husband, an English musician. Their two grown sons lived in Havana, where they engaged in revolutionary activities against the Batista dictatorship. In 1958 one of the sons was arrested and tortured almost to death. His parents went to Havana to try to do something for him, and when they returned to Oriente they found that the rebels had occupied their property and would not permit them to set foot on it, not even to get clothes. In June of 1958 they started out on a peregrination through the Sierra Maestra in search of Fidel Castro to ask for justice, but were unable to catch up with him. The couple wandered about looking for him until Batista fell; then they went to Havana, obtained an order of restitution, and returned to their hacienda. But the Rebel Army still refused to allow them to enter their house.

They had to start living off the generosity of their friends. Nevertheless, they did not want to make a scandal or to complain about the revolution, and tried every amicable means at their disposal by going to the authorities. When they appeared in my office, I put them in contact with Raúl Castro, who ordered an investigation. The occupant military chief was brought to Havana under arrest, and the couple returned to my office, filled with faith, to give thanks. Their joy was premature, however. The property was never returned to them. It was being held because its coffee harvest was a rich one, and the time for getting it in was drawing near. At the investigation ordered by Raúl Castro it was reported that the man was "a feudal master," that he had a stock for imprisoning peasants, and so on. Even if this were true, it did not give the government the right to expropriate his wife's property. When we left for Washington they still could

205

not return to their house. One month later, agrarian reform and the official redistribution of all such cultivated lands put an end to their hopes.

Such was the picture in Cuba, in April 1959, when we made our trip to the United States.

chapter

14

The trip to the United States was the result of an invitation extended by the American Society of Newspaper Editors. The invitation was transmitted by Jules Dubois. After some vacillation, Fidel agreed to sign the paper engaging him to attend the society's luncheon in April 1959. The reasons for accepting the invitation were many. Fidel wanted the industrialization of Cuba. Cordial relations would inspire confidence in private investors interested in establishing new industries there. Moreover, the U.S. government appeared to have a feeling of guilt in regard to the Cuban revolution and to the past. It was the moment to erase bad memories and to obtain such things as aid for industrialization, commercial improvement, and a more lenient tariff arrangement.

Our ambassador in Washington called me from that city to ask me if Fidel, now that he was going to the United States, wished an official invitation from the government, and if he should make a gesture in that direction. Fidel said no. He said it was so common for the "sold-out" presidents and dictators to do this that he preferred not to go in the capacity of official guest. That this was his decision is certain. But it is no less certain that not the slightest initiative was taken on the Washington side. If Fidel had been invited, he would have accepted in spite of what he had said; but he could not go looking for an invitation.

That trip was the last opportunity the U.S. government had to attract Fidel with a policy of friendship and rapprochement, for although it is true that interests were even then trying to provoke animosity in Cuba toward the United States, it is also true that Fidel went to the United States full of hope. He was in a good mood and accessible on the trip—but was not approached officially by anyone; nor did he receive a single offer of aid to Cuba.

Fidel's public relations on the trip were handled by a company that had not even competed with the others. Its director, Bernard Relling, came to Havana for a conference with Fidel which took place in my suite. On that day Fidel came down a little before the others, and, with only Isabel present, we were able to converse for ten minutes without interruption. I had noticed a few Communists hanging around him. Though at least visibly they were few and of minor importance, I related to Fidel the experiences of the past. I described the part the Communist Party had played in overthrowing the first nationalistic government Cuba had ever had, that of Grau and Guiteras in 1934, and all the consequences of their actions. He listened in silence, nodding his head, then said:

"Besides, they don't buy anything from us and the United States buys our sugar."

He assured me that he had no intention of making any treaties with Russia, and that he was going to the United States "open to any offers of help in the industrialization of Cuba."

But his aggressiveness, his desire to maintain exalted crusades, the constant influence of his brother and Guevara, the lack of official and efficient U.S. co-operation, and the crafty (and very efficient) infiltration of Communist ideas contributed to a course of action, on our return, that was very different from the one he had expressed to me that afternoon when, far from speaking of austerities, he even said, as he contemplated the beautiful view of Havana from my terrace, that it was fair enough that we should live well, "because after all we have made enough sacrifices."

Relling handled Fidel more astutely than anyone else I had ever seen and obtained unusual co-operation from him. Two of his requests, however, went unsatisfied. I was in complete agreement with Relling on both counts, but Celia was opposed. One was that the men have their hair cut (Fidel's was short); the other was that he select as his guard for the trip those rebel soldiers who had a university background and who spoke English, of whom there were quite a few in the Rebel Army.

In the general conversation that followed the conference, someone mentioned a person by the name of Lilia. Like one coming out of the distant past, but without a trace of emotion, Fidel turned to me and said, "And that Lilia of Mexico, what ever became of her?" Then he turned back and resumed his conversation as if it had nothing whatever to do with him. He had removed her from his life and all but completely from his memory, and he hardly paid any attention to my brief reply: "She is well. She is still there."

It was the only time Fidel ever came to my suite, and I took advantage of the opportunity to corner him, before he could leave, and get him to pay the latest bills that had accumulated at the Hilton. It was even an amusing scene. I stood in the doorway with arms outstretched to keep him from leaving, and to give the cashier, who had received a message from Isabel to hurry to my suite, time to get there. Relling looked on in astonishment at my last-ditch effort to get the bill paid and the adventurers tossed out. But Fidel was in excellent humor that day. He ran toward my bedroom to make his escape through another door, but the man was already there with the bills in his hand. The sum involved this time, and it was the third payment, was $56,000. Fidel was greatly surprised at the amount. And only then was I authorized to force those adventurers, who had been happily ensconced at the Hilton for three months without ever having been invited, either to leave the hotel or assume responsibility for their own bills.

I have never worked harder, longer, or more frantically than I did preparing that trip. With Isabel absent for a whole week, I had to answer by myself the deluge of long-distance calls that came day and night from people all over the United States and Canada who insisted that Castro include their club, university, or private home in his itinerary. (One invitation was to the Strawberry Festival in Florida!) I could not seek relief by disconnecting the phones at night, because our ambassadors in Washington and the United Nations were constantly calling for information and a list of the names of those who would be in Fidel's party, so that they could arrange invitations and accommodations in the hotels I had selected (Fidel did not want luxury hotels). Unfortunately, it was never possible for me to furnish such a list, for it kept growing every day. Although he had already approved the official list, which we had agreed would not contain more than twenty persons, Fidel sent me every reporter, friend, or employee who expressed a desire to go along, until the total was raised to seventy. (Most of them went on to Canada and South America with Fidel, and were given open expense accounts in hotels and bars, plus $200 each for pocket money.) In addition to all this, I had to chase around getting passport photographs of Fidel, Celia, and the guard, and obtain passports for everybody, while continuing the normal functions of my office.

I knew that there would be many more than seventy showing up at the airport, suitcase in hand, ready to add themselves to the list of passengers. With the chief of the FAR (Rebel Air Force), Pedro Luis Díaz Lanz, I decided that our Britannia and the military plane carrying the newspapermen would leave from the Camp Libertad airfield instead of the civil airport at Rancho Boyeros. On the morning of our departure I announced through press and radio that we were leaving from Rancho Boyeros; then I informed each person on the list that the announcement was a decoy—we had stationed soldiers at the entrance of the FAR airfield—and I told Fidel our point of departure only two hours before the time scheduled for the take-off.

I must state that Fidel did not send me any Communists for inclusion on the roster. I would have balked at that, for the American press was already pinning a Red label on us that we had as yet done nothing to deserve. I did not want to give the press a chance to build up a "case" against us.

Although Fidel showed up at the airport two hours late (while a special reception committee with all its protocol was waiting for us in Washington); although when he did appear it was in a worn and wrinkled uniform and with dirty nails that I had to clean personally on the plane, while he read comic books; although he lost his temper a few times in Washington when I would not let him stop to speak in any but the prearranged places, from the moment he set foot on American soil he became punctual, neat, and pleasant. The cordiality of the American public tamed that young lion and brought out the friendliest side of his nature.

Our arrival in Washington coincided with President Eisenhower's departure for a few days of golf, a fact which naturally received much publicity. Vice-President Nixon had a private, unofficial interview with Fidel for half an hour. We never learned what was said, but it seems that the conversation did not go beyond the light chatter char-

211

acteristic of a courtesy call. Fidel was also received by a congressional committee. What he had told me before about not coming to the United States as a mendicant, he emphasized in his public appearances in Washington and in New York. Dr. Rufo López Fresquet, who for more than a year was Fidel's Minister of the Treasury (today he is an exile), told me recently that Fidel instructed him "not to go around asking for anything" during our visit. But, as I have already said, Fidel was hoping for offers which he never received. Knowing his hopes and his pride, it is certain that this vexed him greatly.

Dr. López and I were beside Fidel in all his Washington press conferences. Fidel asked to have me next to him at the Society of Newspaper Editors luncheon, and in order to include me, Jules Dubois had to change the seating arrangements on the dais at the last moment. Fidel did the same at the National Press Club luncheon, where the tradition of not seating women on the presidium was broken. These arrangements enabled me to continue my work of helping Fidel, at his signal, when he came under the concentrated fire of the newspapermen in the rapid and dynamic question-and-answer periods (four hundred at the Society of Newspaper Editors luncheon, six hundred at the National Press Club luncheon). I realized that it was a delicate moment in Cuban-American relations. We were in "hostile" territory. Because of "Operation Truth" and the new laws we had passed, and because of the fear of radicalism that plagues the American economic interests, the press in the United States was especially watchful and critical.

Owing to my constant nearness to Fidel, and the nature of my work, the one most talked about in the newspapers, after Fidel, was me. My personal appearance, and that of my friend and secretary, Isabel, was commented on favorably. (One article referred to us as "Dior-like dressed ladies.") In almost all the photographs taken of Fidel in

Washington I appeared at his side. When the journalists who had been to the Sierra Maestra during the war were decorated with gold medals at our embassy, Fidel and I performed the ceremony. The result of all this was that I incurred the displeasure of those who worked with him, and particularly of the women, who began to advise Fidel that I had gone along for the fun of it, to enjoy myself and dress up in fine clothes.

One day I invited Fidel to join me on a visit to the National Gallery. I thought a brief immersion in the world of art might have a calming effect on him, and possibly elevate him from his primitive existence and the philistinism of those who surrounded him. He said he would like to go, but he was too busy. I think that for once he really meant it, because of the different environment he was in. Nevertheless, when he asked for me and was told that I had gone to the art museum he was annoyed, because, unlike the others—who had no life, no possibilities independent of Fidel Castro—I was not placing myself at his disposal day and night like a willing slave. The others took advantage of his annoyance and my absence to make malicious remarks, and Fidel ended by believing some of them. The attentions I received in Washington, and again in Canada, did not help matters; Fidel is very jealous of his "star"status.

Fidel's secretary was a woman who had worked for the volatile Eduardo Chibás. Fidel had obtained her from the Ministry of Foreign Affairs shortly after I had started working with him. I had known her since she was fourteen, considered her almost a member of my family, and had been delighted to have her become a member of our little team. Although I find it very hard to believe, I have had proof that she too joined in the malicious chorus that put me in a bad light in Fidel's eyes. Another participant in that ignoble chorus, and one of the most zealous, was not a woman but a man—the director of the Cuban newspaper *Revolución*. He protested furiously that I was "the one who was always in the photographs with Fidel." This person, a former proofreader to whom I had offered my friendship and hospitality in Mexico, had become an "important" person after the victory and then czar of the Cuban press. He selected his editorial staff from among unknown writers and amateur journalists whose resentfulness was so strong that his newspaper has been one of the fountains of hate and angry aggressiveness in our country.

Revolución became such a negative organ that a friend of mine who read it every morning at breakfast called it *"Bonjour Tristesse."* I refused all requests to contribute to that harmful newspaper. Before our trip to the United States, and at a time when so many stressed their contributions to the revolution in articles and television interviews, I had never spoken or written about my role. Nor had I tried to insert myself in Fidel's photographs or accompany him in his personal appearances before the public. Such was not my job. In the United States it was.

On our arrival in New York, an immense crowd shoved and strained and shouted for Fidel all the way from Grand Central Station to the Statler Hotel. Suddenly Fidel wanted to get out of the automobile. He wanted to greet the people from the middle of the street. The two State Department detectives and I insisted that he stay in the car, but his secretary, instead of helping to calm him down, incited him to go ahead, saying, "He has to greet his public." Celia agreed with her, and the next thing we knew, Fidel had jumped out on the street from the slowly moving automobile. Instantly there was bedlam as the crowd became an uncontainable mob that surged toward him, even getting under the horses of the mounted policemen.

When I saw that mob came swarming toward the automobile I was glad for the safety button on the door beside me. Of course Fidel had to return immediately to the automobile, which for a moment I thought might be overturned. Although he did not admit it, I am sure he understood that he had behaved badly. Several persons were injured, and I made certain, without commenting, that he was apprised of the fact when the incident was described in the evening papers. It was one of his few lapses into bad manners during the trip, although the same thing happened later at Princeton University, again with the complicity of his secretary and Celia, and we barely escaped being crushed by a thousand seemingly crazed students.

Our arrival in New York coincided with that of several Cuban Communists of press and radio, along with a woman who was a well-known Communist intrigante and one of Fidel's most persistent goaders. They were sent by Vilma Espín, Raúl Castro's wife. Yanes and I had more or less expected something of the sort, and Yanes brought along several friends of his with the object of guarding Fidel closely. We agreed that none of those Communists must be allowed to slip into any of Fidel's public appearances or photographs. It was easy to see what they were up to. Fidel was developing a cordial attitude toward the United States. He had begun to formulate a humanistic policy that threatened to upset the design which the Communists had been tracing ever since Che Guevara, as military chief of La Cabaña, had introduced troop indoctrination and recommended two women Communists for high positions in government institutions.

Fidel was pleased with the way the trip was going. He was agreeable and accessible, and he listened to advice. Frank Bartholomew, the president of UPI, who had waited a week in Havana without being able to see Fidel (who was in another province at the time), was brought by Relling to greet Fidel in New York, and they had a friendly chat. He was a very fine man and I was glad that he had his interview at last. Fidel even agreed to an interview with Mr. Luce, several of whose publications had been attacking us rather severely. Then, the night before he was to speak to the Latin Americans in Central Park, he had a call from his brother in Cuba, who took it upon himself to "inform" Fidel that in Cuba it was "being said" that he had "sold out to the Americans." Fidel almost wept. He demonstrated to his companions that he had not made a single unworthy or submissive speech (which was true).

*　　*　　*

It was in Washington that I decided to marry the young American writer. His amorous attentions had reached a peak with my arrival in Washington, and from that point on he was the only one I could turn to for relief from the constant harassments of Fidel's envious entourage on the one hand and the silent but efficient Communist phalanx on the other. Although on the exterior I had my share of gratifications and honors, it was he who was finally my only truly pleasant and soothing influence, and who kept me from sinking into utter exhaustion and despondency. He offered what appeared to be a firm, stable love, and what a woman most needs in life: protection.

I do not think politics is a reasonable career for a woman, much less an unattached woman. I was beginning to see that for all the good will Celia Sánchez might have for me, and for all my attempts to assure her of her primary position alongside Fidel (in my interviews I was always careful to give prominence to her and to Fidel's secretary), any influence I might continue to have on Cuba's behalf with respect to Fidel could best be served by my getting married. An unattached woman, unless she is a scarecrow, is bound to make other women uneasy. At the same time I decided to relinquish my job with the government. Breaking all official ties would not only enable me to have a private life but would put me in a better position, perhaps, to counsel Fidel from outside the circle of his "court," where advisers rose and fell with ease, or maintained their positions by means of absurd juggling acts. In any case I considered it a good moment to leave, for, with Fidel triumphant and apparently embarked on a peaceful, constructive policy, I felt that the success of my labor was at highest point.

Because excessive trips, cables, and long-distance calls had put my fiancé's budget out of kilter, we would not be able to marry and set up housekeeping in New York before autumn. It was he who had the idea of my switching to the United Nations, although he assured me that he could support me quite well through his own work and that if I had to lose my position as ambassador it would make no difference to him. Knowing Fidel, I said that I would not ask for that transfer under any circumstances, that if he wished he could make the request on his own. He also wanted to go to Cuba to ask my parents for my hand. Amused, I declared that the one he ought to ask was Fidel Castro, who was about to lose my services. My fiancé took this literally, and on the train that carried us from New York to Boston, where Fidel was to speak at Harvard, he waited in line for the chance to see Fidel alone, while I waited in the next car expecting to hear the roar of the "dragon." I was about to become the first one to leave him, and I knew how possessive he is and that desertion is one of the things that irritate him most.

My writer returned very pleased. He had asked Fidel for permission to marry me, and had also asked if he would transfer me to the United Nations. Fidel, he said, had told him very serenely that love was free, that it was indifferent to nationality, and that it was natural for us to want to be married.

However, from that moment on I could not have existed less for Fidel if I had died. When I went to his car, he spoke to me very briefly, calmly and distantly, without looking at me, and said in a low and utterly toneless voice that he would have to consult the Minister of Foreign Affairs about my transfer, as he did not wish it to be thought that he was favoring me in matters relating to my personal career. We were facing each other with only a narrow table between us, but he seemed miles away and he did not look at me.

In Montreal Fidel was given a banquet by fifty businessmen, who made us a gift of a fine tractor, and I made the little speech of thanks in French—without, I hope, too many mistakes. Earlier in the evening the toastmaster began the proceedings by raising his glass in a toast to the two Chiefs of State: the Queen of England and the President of Cuba. Fidel, thinking the toast was to him, explained to the gathering, "But I am not the President of Cuba . . ." I think he realized by the toasts that followed that he had made a *faux pas,* although no one said anything to him about it. There was of course nothing shameful about a new revolutionary ruler's being unaware of details of ceremonial protocol, just as there was nothing shameful in his inability to express himself in French, as those gentlemen wished him to do, but I think he was deeply chagrined by his slip.

The itinerary which I had prepared for him, and which he had approved, called for us to resume our journey to Quebec and Toronto the following morning. But that night, after the banquet, I learned that Fidel had changed his plans. Without a word to me, he had canceled our visits to those cities and was leaving instead for Buenos Aires, to speak in Cuba's name at an international economic conference that was in progress there. Fidel, his secretary, and Celia had made up a list of those who were to accompany him in the Britannia, and my name was not on it. I learned this not from Fidel, nor from Celia, but from the comparative stranger (a friend of Celia's who had joined us in New York) who was replacing me in my duties for the rest of the trip. It was she who told me that she was collecting the passports of those who were on the list, in order to obtain visas. She had come not to collect my passport but to give me the money for my ticket to Cuba on a commercial airliner. The rest were returning to Cuba on the military plane.

I could not believe my ears and rushed to Fidel's suite. I found him alone in the dining room, and told him that I wished to continue working with him until I left for the United Nations, and asked him to change his mind about not taking me along to South America. He replied that he never went back on a decision, turned his back, and left the room.

It was at that moment, in reality, that our lives separated. I understood the nature of his wound, but his action hurt me deeply because I was very fond of him, and that tearing asunder of our close relationship caused me even greater sadness than did my renunciation a year and a half later.

chapter

15

At the very moment that I entered the house of my parents, the day after my return from Canada, Fidel's Britannia could be heard flying over Havana and his voice came over the radio in a brief salutation to the Cuban people from the plane. My parents had thought me on that plane; they did not know that I had been back at the Hilton since the day before. Their eyes filled with tears as they saw me standing in the doorway. They understood something was wrong.

I tried to make light of my sudden return. I emphasized my marriage plans and the security I was going to have. It was a good time to make them accept the idea of my leaving Cuba once again. They were unhappy about that and also about my leaving Fidel, for, like the rest of the Cuban people at that time, they felt great affection for him. I had never made an attempt to introduce them to him, primarily because I was unwilling to tamper with their illusions. Admiration, I well knew, is best preserved at a distance. For my parents, therefore, Fidel was still a living legend.

While Fidel was on his meteoric tour of South America (it lasted a week and brought mental and physical exhaustion to his companions), I wrote an article that was published in the magazine *Bohemia*. It was entitled "Outcome of a Trip" and was the only article I wrote while I was with the government. In it I tried to stimulate Fidel and bind him more closely to his promises by holding up the humanist policy he had formulated, and the enthusiastic reception both he and that policy had received from everybody. I closed with a fond farewell to my island from one who would soon be off once again to serve it in a foreign land; and with a good-by to Fidel, asking him to govern Cuba with "the white rose in his hand." This was the symbol José Martí had created to represent love, friendship, and the absence of spite. (The exiled *batistianos*, with typical irreverence and shamelessness, later took the name of their organization from this symbol.)

Although I was still nominally working for Fidel, I did not go to pay him my respects when he returned. On that day there was an enormous rally in the Civic Plaza, at which the Cuban people showed their satisfaction with Cuba's friendship with the United States. The Plaza could be seen from my terrace, and I watched the rally while I heard the speeches on the radio. When Fidel praised his escort of rebels, he referred to "the humble soldiers who are not from the university, who are not doctors of philosophy, nor do they speak French; but they are loyal and have always been with me." The arrow was aimed straight at me.

A few days later, in a television appearance, he annoyed the Communists considerably when he asserted with angry emphasis: "Understand me well, gentlemen— this is not a red revolution, it is an olive-green revolution!" And he ordered the unions not to allow the Communists to take over the influential positions.

On the same day that my article appeared in *Bohemia*, Fidel's son was injured almost fatally in an automobile accident. When they were trying to locate Fidel, it was to me that they telephoned. I called Yanes at his suite, and Fidel was there. Then I called the best surgeon in Havana and asked him to rush to the Emergency Hospital. When

I got there, the doctor was already at the boy's side. They would have to remove his spleen. Fidel was waiting in a small room with President Urrutia and his wife. He looked at me silently and with despair. He sat motionless, leaning forward. In a low, grief-filled voice he began to deplore his having given the boy wild youths for chauffeurs. I touched his arm and could not prevent a tear from falling on his sleeve. Fidelito's condition at that moment was critical, and I was thinking how cruel it would be for my friend if he lost his only child. It seemed we were fated to be brought together by misfortune. The only thing I said to him was, "I am here beside you if you need me, as I always have been." That night the boy was in an oxygen tent, and his mother joined Fidel at his bedside. I think it was the first time in many years that Fidel and his ex-wife were able to speak together for a few moments without the rancors and grievances of the past.

The operation was successful, and the boy recovered. My relations with Fidel reverted to what they had been before the accident. Despite the brief encounter at the hospital, I preferred not to see him again. His recent trip had satisfied the news services for the time being, and at the end of May 1959 few people came from abroad to see him. Those who did arrive I sent over with Isabel. According to the Minister of Foreign Affairs, I would be transferred to the United Nations in September, when the General Assembly reconvened. Until then my position in Cuba would continue to be an awkward one. Then I received an unexpected invitation to attend the drama festival at Epidaurus, Greece. The Minister authorized me to leave officially on a cultural mission, and Isabel, whose position as my assistant was voluntary and thus unofficial (she lived off her rents), decided to accompany me. I handed over the files to the officials who would henceforth be discharging my duties for the Premier. I did not see Fidel, nor did I ask his permission. As far as I was concerned, he had stopped being my boss when he had dismissed me in Canada. I sent him a verbal message of farewell via his secretary, and on a post card I sent her from Crete I included regards for him.

During that summer of 1959 Isabel and I traveled mostly around the Mediterranean. We visited Portugal, Morocco, France, Italy, Greece and its islands, Turkey, Iran, Lebanon, Egypt, and returned through Switzerland and England. With that trip, and especially in Greece, I returned to my harmonious world from out of that elemental one in which I had been immersed for three years. Strength and joy and peace seeped back into me. The wounds of Mexico and the thorny tangles of power seemed unequal to a single column of the Parthenon. I have heard many cries of "viva!" in this world, and sometimes it has come from my lips, but never with more emotion than when I found myself before Pallas Athene.

On the ship that took us from Corfu to the port of Patras we came across a discarded newspaper that had a large picture of Fidel on the front page, under a banner headline. We could make out just two words: "Castro" and "Cuba." In despair that something serious had happened, we went from port to starboard looking for someone to translate for us, and finally learned that Castro had deposed the President of Cuba, Manuel Urrutia. It was the beginning of the overt absolutism that subsequently matured into the present tyranny.

I am not given to calumny, and I never attribute anything to anyone without being absolutely certain of my information. And so I shall produce verbatim a statement made by Mr. Victor Riesel in an article in the New York *Daily Mirror* of August 27, 1959. The article, entitled "Red Chinese Infiltrate Cuba," ends in this way: "Recently, for example, one of Fidel Castro's secretaries, Teresa Casuso, returned to Havana from Peiping. She anounced that China's commune system was the right way for Cuba." The absurdity of such a statement is underscored by the fact that I have never been in a Communist country, except for a sight-seeing tour of Berlin which traditionally takes tourists through both West and East Berlin.

I arrived in Cuba in September, and five days later was in New York. Once again, I did not look for Fidel or say good-by to him. Before I left for New York, Cuban Airlines gave me the job of supervising their public relations in that city.

Then followed several months of active participation at the United Nations. The many people who heard my numerous interventions there can testify that I always tried to win friends for my country, whose aspirations I continued to uphold without, however, giving offense to anyone. I spent some very pleasant hours in the admirably calm, deliberate atmosphere of that international organism, and learned much, and made friends from all over the world. I remember those friends with affection even as I think they may remember me. Yes, I feel nostalgia for the relaxed tempo of that place beside the East River where men from every part of the world try to co-ordinate the opposed interests of the nations in the universal aspiration for peace.

In November of that year there was disquieting news from Cuba once again. An analysis of the trajectory of Fidel's rule—one can even say of his life—shows that a definitive deviation took place in that month. It was in November that his order to the unions to prevent the Communists from seizing the influential positions was countermanded. It followed the imprisonment of his old comrade Hubert Matos and the mysterious disappearance of his friend Camilo Cienfuegos, chief of the Rebel Army. It preceded the appointment of Raúl Castro as head of all the armed forces and Che Guevara's installation as president of the National Bank of Cuba. Fidel Castro had thrown in his lot with the Communists. Even while I was upholding the highest ideals of the Cuban people, those ideals were being handed over to their own natural enemy by him who had proclaimed himself their guardian.

Although I was still very fond of my fiancé, I kept putting off the wedding. The prospect of married life seemed less enticing from close by. I went home for the Christmas holidays. At ten o'clock on New Year's Eve I went to greet Yanes in his suite at the Hilton. Yanes told me that Fidel was there, in one of the rooms, and that I should stay and say hello. (It was evident that Fidel was with a female visitor.) Then a door opened and Fidel came out. I expected a resumption of that resentful remoteness, but the affection we had once felt for each other won out. He had not received me better the day I had arrived from Mexico. His face brightened and he said with pleased surprise, "What, you here?" He opened his arms and we embraced each other gladly. He added affably, "I've seen a sweater over at Celia's . . ." (I had sent Christmas gifts for him and Celia to Celia's house.) Then he cried, "Come, come with me!"

We went to the house where Celia lived with her sisters. He kept his clothes there, and he was going to dress up in full uniform. I was invited to see in the new year with him at a huge dinner being given at the Hilton. Celia did not want to go, though she was in evening dress, by which I supposed that she had been waiting for him to return from his escapade. But she showed not the slightest irritation. We chatted while Fidel changed, and she asked me in a very sympathetic way about my life in New York, and what had happened with the marriage. When I told her that I had been postponing it she said I had done right not to marry, that freedom was better. However much I urged her to come to the dinner, she insisted that she was tired, and remained with her sisters and other friends.

On our way to the Hilton I told Fidel that I had sent him—by way of his secretary, who either had not received it or had not given it to him—a whole page out of one of the New York newspapers with large photographs of various world figures. His was at the top, opposite that of Montgomery, and the heading (it was an ad) read: "The World Loves a Victor." With that childish quality he had not yet lost he was as interested in that as if it were the first time he had ever been mentioned abroad. I think he did not yet fully realize the extent of his fame, in spite of the fact that his ambition—never expressed in words— was to be *the* Latin American leader, a new Simón Bolívar.

As our automobile approached the hotel, the crowd thickened around it, so that it could scarcely inch forward. People clung to the car in bunches to shake his hand, and a few old women even kissed it. One woman pushed through the crowd, caught hold of his hand, and said, shaking and crying, "I have an incurable illness and I did not want to die without shaking your hand." And she kissed it, as one does the hand of a saint.

Surrounded by his guard, we entered the lobby and managed to get to the elevator. I say "managed" because it took us half an hour to get there. He asked me if I wished to go to my room to change, which surprised me; it was a sign of his progress in social etiquette, or at least of his acceptance of the kind of woman I am. But I remembered the waves of resentment my dresses and hats had caused in Washington, and preferred to wear the simple black dress I had on. One thing he did not do, at any time, was to mention my life abroad, or the uncelebrated wedding, or the man I had consented to marry.

He seated me at his small table, where the only other Cuban was the President of the Republic, Osvaldo Dorticós. The others were Joe Louis, Jean Paul Sartre's secretary and his wife, the Italian screen writer Cesare Zavattini, and a Negro editor from the United States. Together we awaited the arrival of the new year. It was certainly a far cry from the cold loneliness of the room in Mexico where I had spent my last New Year's Eve. So many people came from the other tables, holding out menus for Fidel to sign, that the waiters could not get through to serve us, and at midnight we still had nothing to toast the new year with. While the human wall around us shouted on and on, Fidel, at that precise moment, smiled at me and said, "If I don't go insane this year it will be because God is very great."

I am thinking now of that sentence by Euripides: "Whom the gods would destroy they first make mad." And in this hour of remembering, in these first days of another new year, I cannot stop feeling anguish for that friend blinded by the gods of anger and violence, like tragic Orestes assailed by the Furies, or Macbeth, around whom the cackling witches danced. For once again we have come a long way in the space of one year. As I sat with Fidel into the first hours of 1960, listening to Cubans shout his praises, I was still hopeful, I did not believe it could be so sad a year as it has been for Cuba, and that before it was over so many of us would have had to separate ourselves from him and from the dream to build a nation of liberty and kindness together.

Not long after I returned to New York my engagement was dissolved, and a week later I went as Cuban representative to a conference in Buenos Aires arranged by the United Nations. I went by ship and stopped off at Rio de Janeiro, which was in the middle of its annual carnival romp. After the conference I traveled through the rest of South America, learning my own continent. In those Indo-Hispanic countries I continued to speak on behalf and in praise of Cuba, for I still had faith in the good will of my friends and their laws "for the improvement of the people's condition." One of the loveliest memories of my life will always be Bolivia, where the Indian women carried me enthusiastically from the crowded rally and kissed me and gave me gifts and had me join them in their graceful folk dance, the *huaino*.

I returned to New York, and two weeks later I was back in Cuba to report on the Buenos Aires conference, and on what I had observed in the various countries I had visited. It was now June 1960. I felt silence all around me. My friends seemed afraid to talk. I began to investigate, and now I saw the results of the revolutionary government's one and a half years of power. All that I had feared was now happening. Fidel had become a dictator. *Les enfants au pouvoir* went from bad to worse, making one mistake after another. The country was divided into three groups —those for the government, those against, and the confused majority in the middle.

I learned that Captain Yanes was in prison. He had been there since April and was being held incommunicado, although no charge had as yet been made against him. I could not see him, but I could try to talk to Fidel on behalf of our friend. The telephone operators at the Hilton helped me with all their gracious diligence. On the day before I was to leave for New York I got a call from one of them, informing me that at that moment Fidel was at Celia's. Celia had changed her phone number several times in my absence, and the girls could not give me the new one, but they passed on my messages.

I went to Celia's house. It was raining. There were new guards downstairs. I knew only one of them. They enforced their regulations strictly. Whoever brought a message upstairs, I learned, was punished with three days in the guardhouse. It was raining very hard, and I waited outside for some time, then went to the public phone on the corner and asked the girls at the Hilton to inform

Celia that I was waiting below. Still there was no response, and finally I went back to the hotel. When my father came to see me that evening, I told him many things neither he nor my mother had been aware of, and that I was thinking of renouncing. I did not step out of the hotel that night, but there was no reply from Celia to the messages I had sent her. If I had managed to see Fidel that time I might well have wound up in La Cabaña prison, like Yanes.

Since the first outbreak that day at the Hilton, before the trip to the United States, the quarreling between Celia and Yanes had increased proportionately to Fidel's reliance on Yanes. Little by little the private war had come into the open and had culminated in the "fall into disgrace" of the captain, who had few friends among the "rebel élite." He was seized and imprisoned by orders of Raúl Castro, and treated with shameful arbitrariness. Fidel's ingratitude and disloyalty in permitting Yanes to be got rid of in this matter, and his complicity afterwards when Yanes appealed to him for protection, caused my own bond of loyalty to Fidel to begin to fray.

My parents were waiting for me at the airport when I arrived there the next day. They were sad and nervous and showed signs of age and illness, they who had been so healthy and handsome a couple. My mother still believed in "the revolution." She cried and asked me not to cut myself off from what had been my whole life, to wait. She said there were many good things to save, that they had also done much good. It was the first time in all my political life that she asked me to change an opinion or tried to influence my thought. I knew it was not for the sake of convenience. Because of me, and in worse times, my father had many times lost his job; instead of reproaching me, they had always encouraged me not to waver in my ideals. Seeing them so alone and unprotected, still suffering the consequences of my activities, I remembered the many troubles, upheavals, and separations I had involuntarily caused them. I promised my mother I would wait for a while and look at the whole picture as objectively, and the government side of the picture as sympathetically, as I could without compromising my conscience.

Before take-off, the police came on the plane and made three persons leave; only one returned. I myself had boarded the plane with the greatest facility and official consideration. I had the awful sensation of being on the ugly, the unjust side. I felt like a persecutor, a police official. I looked at the anxious passengers and was ashamed, and blushed for my privileges. No, this was not for me. I could not possibly go on like this.

In New York I condemned myself to muteness so that I could keep my promise to my mother without betraying my conscience. I told myself that others were going through worse things, and made up a story about having something wrong with my larynx and having been ordered by doctors in Cuba not to speak for several months. In this way I avoided having to defend the government in interviews, university talks, appearances on television, at conferences, and so forth. Shortly afterwards, our Minister of Foreign Affairs, Dr. Raúl Roa, whom I have known all my life, came to New York, and my internal conflicts grew even more complicated. Not only did he show himself to be full of faith in the government, but he spoke to me of its triumphs, of increases in agricultural production, in employment opportunities, in purchasing power among the majority of the population; he spoke of the "maneuvers" of the selfish interests who had been hurt by the reforms, their preparations for a counter-revolution....

Worst of all, at a meeting he called for the delegation,

Roa told us that the editor of the exiles' magazine, *Bohemia Libre,* had sent him a proposition: both he and the chief of the Cuban mission were promised $40,000 each if they renounced. The ambassadors were offered $10,000; and all the delegates were guaranteed their monthly salary of $2,000. All this, according to Roa, was to come out of a fund raised by the U.S. government. Naturally, anyone thinking of renouncing would automatically stop short on hearing such a thing, for fear of being classified as "bought," although the truth is that he is giving up his privileges and his income by taking that step. Roa spread that report far and wide, and in Cuba it was given a great deal of publicity. It grieves me to think that there are people in Cuba who may have been deceived by that announcement, and who may, in all good faith, think that I was "bought" when I finally did separate myself from the government.

In the midst of all these anxieties and conflicts of conscience I decided, after a month of sign language and written notes (and an occasional articulated sentence that escaped me), to get away for what was left of the summer. I quickly arranged a trip to the Far East which, despite Mr. Victor Riesel, I had not yet seen, and which in the end became a trip around the world.

When I went to say good-by to my companions at the Cuban delegation, the reply to my request for a leave of absence had not yet arrived from Cuba. The chief of the mission was worried and insisted that I postpone or cancel the trip, as going off without permission was cause for dismissal. But that was what I wanted. Speaking in a whisper, I told them that I was leaving the next morning with or without permission. I refused to put through a call to Roa in Havana asking for authorization, as my good Chief (he even offered to pay for the call) insisted. By being dismissed, I hoped to avoid taking the step which my mother so earnestly opposed, and which would enable the regime to call me a "counter-revolutionary."

It did not work. Sometimes it is difficult not to believe in an ironic fate. That night the mission secretary called me to say that the cable had arrived, authorizing me to take a vacation. She sounded relieved. But I felt guilty, for in Cuba they were making everything easy for me, while I wanted to run out on them. . . .

The next morning I left for San Francisco, where Isabel Bermúdez rejoined me. By working miracles with relatives living outside Cuba, and by paying the fare in Cuba (this was still permitted at the time), she was able to arrange an around-the-world trip. No traveler could exit from Cuba with more than $150 (the figure was later cut to $5) and it was necessary to work those "miracles." Isabel is amusing company and I had encouraged her to make the trip with me. Once again I found myself laughing as I had the previous summer. (In a San Francisco restaurant, desiring English muffins, she asked for "English coffins.") We felt happy and free, and far removed from the Cuban anguish we left behind once again like soldiers on furlough. I knew I would have to face it on my return, and tried to reassure myself with the last tiny hope that the difficulties Fidel was starting to have with his people would make him change course in time.

We were in Hawaii, Japan, Hong Kong, then I headed for the Philippines, Cambodia, Thailand, and Burma while Isabel, who was afraid of running out of money, went straight to Bangkok. I was to overtake her in India, but she had already left Calcutta when I arrived there, and we did not meet again until I reached New York. I fell in love with India. There, where spiritual values are so strong, my own spirit strengthened as I felt it withdrawing from all that was not simplicity, internal security, peace. India gave me the strength to do what I had, finally, to do when I arrived back in New York. The serenity it brought is still with me; it enables me to look peace-fully upon those who declare themselves my "enemies."

From India I returned by way of Austria, Germany, and Denmark, and arrived in New York on September 20 for the reopening of the General Assembly.

chapter

16

In New York I learned that Fidel Castro was there and was to speak at the United Nations. I rose early and bought a newspaper. He was staying at the Hotel Theresa in Harlem. Suddenly all that I had against him as a ruler was forgotten. I wanted to run to his side in the hour of his "trouble," when, as I thought, all doors had been closed to him in this city that had previously welcomed and acclaimed him. I was still able to be taken in by his ruses.

I called my office to learn if Fidel would appear at the General Assembly's reopening that morning. The girl who took my call told me that I was no longer on the list of delegates; however, no transfer had been ordered for me and I was still a member of the mission. Furthermore, there was a message for me from Carlos Olivares, the Undersecretary of Foreign Affairs (and the real power in the Foreign Ministry), saying that before I could be accredited as a delegate for the new session I would have to go to Cuba for a talk with him.

I had already had one talk with Carlos Olivares. I had met him in South America that spring, when he was an unknown envoy sent by Raúl Castro to speak to the workers of those countries. In our Chilean embassy we had had a political discussion, though it might more accurately be termed an argument. Then in Japan, on my most recent trip, I had met a woman who was a Communist and a close collaborator of his in the Ministry. She was in Japan to attend one of those international "peace" congresses for which Communists have such a marked weakness, and was astonished that I had not participated, and that I was not going to visit "the People's Republic of China." And in Manila I had given an International Congress of Women Lawyers a wide berth, and had rejected our ambassador's suggestion that I give the lie to the Cuban representative who had uttered some hard truths against the Castro regime. In India, when our ambassador there had asked me about Cuba, my reply had been: "Cuba is at this moment a police state." So I had no doubt that at those levels they were very well aware in Cuba that I was not to be counted on as far as upholding the regime was concerned.

I knew what Olivares wanted to talk to me about. In my work at the UN I had consistently maintained a democratic line of defense. I had little doubt that he intended to lecture me on the subject of our alignment with the Soviet bloc. Or maybe he meant to have me "brainwashed," as it was no secret that I was indisposed to defend or justify the totalitarian policy which my government was embracing. No, to return to Cuba and begin singing the praises of the government and make favorable declarations was out of the question. I refused to obey the order. Here again was a perfect opportunity to be fired.

The verbal message was followed by an official cablegram: "To Dr. Teresa Casuso—Come to Cuba for consultation." The Minister, Raúl Roa, was in New York. I told him I was not going.

Fidel was something else again. I wanted to see him, because I did feel the need to give him my reasons. He greeted me affectionately for a few moments in the Assembly lounge. I told him I wanted to talk to him. He told me to come around to the hotel. There was not the

235

least sign of displeasure in his attitude toward me, which only made things more difficult, and obliged me more than ever to explain to him why I could not go on defending him politically. During the few moments that we spoke together, just before the Assembly session was to begin, the representative from Guinea came over and I interpreted for Fidel in the brief, informal chat that followed. It was the last work I did for him, and I think that at that instant we both remembered my little thank-you speech in French Canada that had annoyed him. This time it was the reverse; he seemed pleased that for a moment something from the past had brought us together again. As for me, I felt awful. Face to face with him, noticing traces of illness in his features (when I asked how he was, he said, "I still don't feel too well"), still ignorant of the facts about the affair of the hotels, I was experiencing a kind of traitor complex. Yes, I thought, it is essential that I tell him outright, face to face, all that I have been finding out about Cuba, and why it is impossible for me to continue.

That afternoon I went to the Theresa. I had to wait a long time in the lobby. Then an old journalist friend who was a member of Fidel's party took me with him to the eighth floor, where Fidel was staying. It was a repetition of my first reception at the Hilton. Again I had to wait a long time in the corridor, sending messages to Celia with everyone I knew who went in. The guards were in civilian clothes, and of them all I knew only one. He was one of the boys who had lived in my house in Mexico when Fidel was in the Sierra Maestra. He was not as friendly as he had been then. He appeared to have a position of utmost confidence, and was greatly preoccupied with the comings and goings of the visitors.

At last Celia told the guards to let me in. But it was only to her room, opposite Fidel's, that I went. In it were two girls and two cooks. The girls were relatives of Celia's and were living in New York. I did not know the cooks, and they had not been in the *sierra,* but they were good, modest souls, and very friendly to me. They gave me food and kept offering me coffee. They prepared the meals on a two-range electric stove, and were helped by the girls, who had a few bitter comments to make about the journalistic treatment they had received. They said that they had slaved to clean up the room in the hotel where they had first stayed, before coming to the Theresa, only to read in the newspapers that they had "left everything dirty and covered with chicken feathers." The present room was a pig-sty, with old, dirty paint, peeling walls, and a bathroom whose toilet did not function properly, and when I saw how hard they worked keeping it clean, I understood that once again the newspapers had lied in order to put them in the worst possible light—when there were so many truths they might have printed! It made me feel closer to them and to that sad sense of defeat which I detected in all those decent, cordial people in the room.

I was there seven hours in all. Between her entrances and exits, Celia told me that Fidel was in conference with Núñez Jiménez, then that he had fallen asleep, exhausted, right after his late lunch. I saw that all his food was prepared personally by Celia, and she did not use the water from the taps. I realized then that the rumor that Fidel had been poisoned in Cuba a short while ago might be true. The girls kept eyeing the neighboring rooftops. The idea was not to rely on the protection of the American police. I smiled to myself as I thought how hard it would have been to make them see that that protection was made, not less, but more conscientious by the nature of Castro's relations with the United States, which more than anything dreaded having something happen to him while he was on American soil.

A Cuban military doctor came in and gave Celia "more

drops for Fidel." They talked about the dosage, and Celia said something from which I gathered that it had something to do with the killing of pain, or the calming of nerves. I felt very depressed, and at that moment of conflicting impulses and emotions, coupled with the many hours I had spent sitting there, I began to have a neuralgic pain in my hip. I had never suffered from sciatica before and was convinced that the origin of the pain was in my emotional state. My nature rebels when I am forced for whatever reason to absorb trouble, and as a rule I only fall ill when my spirits are low or when I am imposing something upon them. Sitting there and thinking thoughts against the Castro regime, I felt like a traitor to such kind and friendly people as the cooks and the two girls and Celia. I had an impulse to go down and buy some flowers for Celia. There was not a single flower in her room. On our previous visit our rooms had been full of flowers.

Celia finally told me that Fidel said that as I was "one of the family" and as he was very tired it would be better to let him rest for the remainder of the day and he would see me later on. My calvary continued, and my neuritis worsened. When I got home I had difficulty getting out of the taxi. Before I went to bed I went looking among the things I had brought back from my last trip for a gift for Celia—my farewell gift.

The next morning I went to the UN, and found Fidel and his suite heading for the South Delegates Lounge, the more tranquil of the two large sanctums reserved for members of the organization. Fidel asked me to go and see if the Assembly meeting was about to start. When I came back and went into the lounge, he was sitting with the President of Poland. With Gomulka and Fidel were an interpreter and a few members of the special delegation Fidel had brought with him. (It was a sizable delegation, and included the G-2 chief and two known

Communist "sympathizers"; all had been accredited as diplomats and delegates.) I went up to him to say that the meeting of the Assembly was not starting yet. Standing there, I was able to hear a little of their conversation.

To my astonishment, the President of Poland was saying very gently (he is a man of gentle manners and very different from the comical crudeness of Khruschev) that "there should be elections in Cuba." He insisted that "the legal forms should never be ignored." Fidel turned to Núñez Jiménez and observed almost mockingly, "They cannot see the reality of Cuba, that nobody wants elections there." With the same refined tone of voice, Gomulka again insisted. Fidel continued to reject his reasoning, and Núñez agreed with him, which made me reflect that if both Fidel and Núñez were indeed Communists, as it was already widely believed, they certainly were dissident ones.

At that moment Fidel's bodyguard, the one who had lived in my house, put his arm around my shoulders and, speaking quietly and excusing himself, told me I could not stay. He said it was "a conference between Chiefs of State and nobody ought to approach them." Had I still been bound to Fidel politically I would have insisted on remaining. As such was no longer the case, I told him I would leave, but that he should withdraw, for I would not leave under anybody's "escort," in view of the fact that Fidel had asked me to bring him some information. A few moments later I left, while the obstinacy of Fidel continued to oppose the persuasive efforts of Gomulka.

I understood from the conversation that there had been no change in Fidel. But the push-and-pull of my internal conflict was not over. Now came his speech. Even I, familiar as I was with his tricks, was affected by his method of mingling known historical facts with arguments that had only the appearance of being true. (I can well understand how my people were so easily taken in.

It would be surprising if it had been otherwise.) He managed to confuse even me, and to make me wonder if I were not turning into a reactionary conservative. I felt that it was more urgent than ever that I speak to him, that he give me some justification for the imprisonment of friends and for the "iron fist" in Cuba. (There had not yet been executions of revolutionaries at that point.) Was it because the revolution had to be saved? It was then that I heard him smooth over and rectify some of his previous unjust accusations, like that of attributing "the bombing of Havana" to Díaz Lanz, the first defector, who had only dropped leaflets from an unarmed plane.

When the session was adjourned, I went over to Celia and they took me along with them in their automobile. I remembered with a pang a similar ride, a little over a year before, in this same city of New York. But instead of the acclamation of thousands of people crowding the sidewalks, and the joyful faces of the automobile's occupants, there were now only whistles and angry shouts as we crossed the city, and the sad silence of the passengers. I knew what Fidel must have been suffering at seeing himself so utterly rejected. At that moment I even thought of changing my mind about quitting them. I was still the battleground of a devastating conflict between the harm I knew was being done to Cuba, and the sentimental attachment I felt for those people with whom I had lived, body and spirit, through so much, through so many vicissitudes, so many of our lives' most important moments. At that point, too, I naïvely thought them the victims of an "aggression" that had "forced" them to take refuge in Harlem.

While Celia, with touching care and devotion, prepared Fidel's lunch, I went out and wandered about in the corridors. I was waiting for him to have his lunch, to see if we could talk afterwards. In conversation with members of his party, I learned that, despite his public

240

complaints about the high room rents in the hotel they had moved from, they were paying more at the Theresa. No one could say how or when Fidel had got the idea of moving to the present hotel. I continued to look into it and discovered the bitter truth that the whole thing had been planned beforehand. He had intended from the start to complain that he was being overcharged at the first hotel, to plant himself with his whole retinue and all their baggage at the United Nations and thus present the spectacle that they had no place to stay, then to move to Harlem in order to give the impression that it was only among the humble and despised people of the United States, the Negroes, that the humble and despised Cubans and their leader were able to find shelter.

Employing the Negroes as a tactical weapon was already becoming an important part of Fidel's over-all strategy in Cuba, where he sought to represent himself as the friend and protector of the oppressed—that is, the Negro and the peasant. He must also have begun to see that he would not be able to expect blind, unquestioning support from the less defenseless, hence more critical, groups. Negroes make up a little over 12 per cent of our population. (The rest, according to the 1953 census, are Europeans, Chinese, and mulattoes. The whites, those of European origin, constitute 72.8 per cent of the population, the Chinese 0.5 per cent, and the mulattoes about 13.5 per cent. There is also some crossbreeding of Chinese and Negroes.) It is a fact that although all races in Cuba enjoyed legally an equality of rights, there was room for improvement as far as the Negro was concerned. There was complete integration in the public schools, government jobs were thoroughly accessible to Negroes, and in most respects there was far less racial prejudice in the Cuban Republic than in other countries with a history of slavery; but there has always been a certain amount of discrimination against the Negro in private, high-salaried employment, and there were always the recreation clubs and private beaches where colored persons were not admitted.

There can be no question that the Negro, as a human being and as a citizen of the country in which he resides, must have full and unconditional equality with the other citizens of his country. This is equally true for the peasant, naturally. It was one of our revolutionary goals. But it is pure demagoguery to affirm that men, because they are Negro, or because they are poor, have special merit to occupy positions for which they may not be prepared. It is demagoguery, and of the most dangerous and destructive kind, to launch these repressed, long-suffering groups into a crusade of spite and hate, as Fidel Castro has done, instead of developing an educational and legislative program in their favor. Castro encouraged the incompetent and resentful in Cuba to seize control with him, and arbitrariness and outrage became the symbols of his government from its highest director down to the lowest subalterns. Lack of preparation and consequent inability to compete led them to despise whatever might represent preparation, learning, and refinement. Offended by these qualities, they react by attacking them, and it is the nature of their attack to go about dirty and longhaired, to be ill-tempered, disrespectful, and violent.

This situation was largely brought about by Fidel Castro's preference for what he called his "loyal men" to those who were more competent. Humble peasants who had come to Havana from places that had never seen a school or a road, where civilization was all but unknown, were designated for duties they were unable to perform. The evidence of their own ineptitude only strengthened the sense of inferiority they already had. The exploitation of this sense of inferiority is the demagogic danger of revolutions, which, if they are propelled by ideals, are also sparked by an urge for revenge that must be carefully watched, guided, and restrained. The leader who rescues a people from injustice and oppression owes it to that people to be free of spite, revenge, and the wish to dominate. Otherwise he will become a tyrant and unleash pent-up hatreds not only in himself and his closest aides but in the people as well. The frustration of feeling oneself to be incompentent changes men into despots who crush others because it is the only way they can enjoy unchallenged superiority. This is what happened with Fidel.

At the Theresa that day, I became convinced that, whether by his design or by hers, Celia was not going to let me through to Fidel. It would have to be somewhere else. I was determined to speak to him before he returned to Cuba. I left the hotel and went to the United Nations, where I met a reporter I knew who had been in the Sierra Maestra to interview Fidel. He was a member of the Fair Play for Cuba Committee and invited me to attend a party the committee was giving for Fidel that same afternoon at the Theresa. Fidel did not come to the UN, and back I went with the reporter to the Theresa.

Many of the members of the Fair Play for Cuba Committee whom I saw at the gathering looked poor, and most were interracial couples. It was moving to see those women spreading out cakes and cookies that they themselves had baked and brought in carefully wrapped packages. The next day I read in the papers about "the packages of food that many different women brought when they visited Castro." (Always that unnecessary lie. The reporters, who almost never left the Theresa lobby, knew very well when they saw those women going up with their packages that there was to be a reception in honor of Fidel in the upstairs lounge.) Fidel would not have put in even his brief appearance at the affair if I had not interceded to get the journalist through to Celia's

243

room so that she could urge Fidel, who was in bed, to go up for a few minutes. It grieved me to see those people there with their fiesta and without their guest of honor. It was like the old days.

Soon after he appeared, I saw that it was the least likely place for me to succeed in having that talk with him, and I did not even bother to approach him. I am not sure he even knew I was there. I kept myself at a distance and watched the small group that surrounded him asking him questions, and after a little while I left.

Time was growing short. They were leaving the next day. That evening, her last in New York, Celia came to my house with her brother and sister-in-law to pick up her gift and see my apartment. She brought me Cuban things—a record, books of Fidel's speeches, Núñez Jiménez's *Geography of Cuba*. (Jiménez too had been very cordial to me. If they had conspired to do so, they could not have better succeeded in filling me to the bursting point with repressed affection and the sensation of guilt.) I said nothing to Celia of what I was thinking; that was for Fidel, and Fidel alone.

Although my neuritis, like my spirit, was going from bad to worse, I returned to the Theresa the next morning, because I knew it was the last chance I would ever have to talk to Fidel in all my life, now that I had decided not to return to Cuba. I could have made arrangements with Celia, had I wished, to go with them to Cuba that afternoon. After all, I had been officially ordered to go. But now Fidel and I were on our separate roads. We had already reached the point of no return.

As the time for their departure drew near, Celia, who was very busy, asked me to try to do something about their plane. The plane had been placed under an embargo by an advertising firm in Miami to which the INIT (National Tourist Industry Institute) of Cuba owed a great deal of money. As I was connected with

244

Cubana Airlines, I was in a position to know that the embargo had nothing to do with the U.S. government. I called the Cuban Mission to the UN. While they were informing me that there had been orders from Fidel not to do anything and that I should check with him to determine if something was being done through other channels, Núñez Jiménez came up to me and said not to do anything, that steps had already been taken. I remembered having seen a light-skinned American Negro in the hotel corridor, some days earlier, who had introduced himself as "Colonel" Julian. Holding some papers in his hand, he had insisted over and over that if Fidel merely signed those papers the embargo would be lifted. Members of Fidel's party had replied that the plane had diplomatic immunity and was not subject to embargo. Finally the chief of the G-2 had come out of a room and thrown him out of the hotel, calling him all sorts of names.

While I was on the phone, Fidel had left for the airport. The Cubans who had been conversing with me during my long waits at the hotel took me along to the airport in one of the automobiles. I was going to say good-by to my friends as one does after a wake when the life force that had unified a group of people is dead. I would go through with it to the end. And if the plane was still under an embargo, the long wait would perhaps give me a chance to speak to Fidel.

At Idlewild, as we passed an open area near the hangars, we heard voices exclaiming, "Fidel is taking off!" My Cuban companions were puzzled. We saw a huge plane standing there, and when I circled round to see who was getting aboard, what I saw was an enormous inscription in Russian letters. Fidel was already inside with his more important friends. The door, exhibiting a great hammer and sickle painted in red, was closed. It was Khruschev's personal plane. The last time Fidel had left the United States, from Boston, our plane had been surrounded by friends and well-wishers waving good-by. I remembered Fidel talking indignantly, rejecting what the American press was starting to say about him: that Cuba was being handed over to a Communist power.

The plane took off immediately. For Fidel it was a one-way trip. I stood motionless, surrounded by some fifteen members of his party who had been left behind with instructions to take the embargoed plane, although there had been room on the Russian plane for all. They did not know what to do next; nobody had been forewarned or advised. They stood in a hangar trembling with cold and without a penny in their pockets; they had spent their last dollars buying gifts for their families. Those men were not Communists, and were nothing to Fidel. But they were Cubans. I could not just walk away from those "greenhorns." I tried to do what I could for them, but my neuritis was getting worse and every step was painful. The airport police ordered them out of the hangar and told them to go to where the detained plane was being held; but nobody knew where that was. The only thing we could find out was that Raúl Roa had been left behind to take care of the matter.

For an hour we wandered through the enormous airport trying to locate the plane. I took them to the offices of Cubana Airlines, where the employees were as much in the dark as we. We continued the search. The sky was overcast; rain had been announced for that afternoon. Finally we came across the Cuban plane, very far away, where the cargo section was located. We were not permitted through the gate. Roa was seated inside the plane in protest. Anyone who entered it was not allowed to leave, and the police would not let me through to talk to Roa even after I had showed them my UN card. I was allowed to use the phone in one of the cargo offices, and

246

called every place I could think of, to no avail. We camped there on the humid turf and waited.

My unhappy compatriots, hungry, sneezing, shivering with cold, complained bitterly about the treatment the U.S. government was giving them in not permitting the plane to leave. I tried to explain that it was not a government matter. I explained about the private embargo. They were there because they were paying for Fidel's tricks and burlesques whose sole purpose was to inject rancor into the people. I told them that no order had been given to do anything about having the embargo lifted. With these statements I was stepping over the dividing line that separated two distinct political positions, and was risking their anger. But I wanted them to know the truth behind what was happening to them—to them, the unhappy sufferers, the ones who always pay the price of Fidel's maneuvers.

Roa left the plane and entered one of the cargo offices. I went in and saw him talking indignantly into a phone. He was speaking to Flores, our *chargé d'affaires* in Washington. He was reproaching Flores for the delay in the negotiations to have the embargo lifted. He hung up the receiver exclaiming disgustedly that nothing at all had been done about it until twenty minutes ago. I understood that, like Celia at the hotel, Fidel Castro's Minister of Foreign Affairs was in the dark about the latest game of the *líder máximo,* who when he arrived in Cuba that afternoon would make a speech condemning "the outrages and aggressions of the United States government" and commiserating with "the unfortunate Cubans who had remained behind and were unable to leave. . . ."

I decided to take the group of Cubans away from there before the rain began to come down. Moreover, night was starting to fall and it was unthinkable to leave them camped there on the ground with their baggage like so many gypsies. I told Roa I would take them to the passengers' waiting room of Cubana. I made them as comfortable as I could, gave them what money I had with me, and set out for home. By now the pain in my hip was such that I was unable to walk. With kindness and affection several of them, almost carrying me, helped me down the stairway from the Cuban office. That was my good-by to my people.

For twelve days I was barely able to get out of bed. My blood pressure fell so low that I had to live on Adrenalin. A young Cuban doctor living in New York treated me. He was a sympathizer of the M26–7 and had once been my pupil in the Cuban elementary school where I had taught for a year. When none of the medicines had any effect, I told him what I thought the trouble was. It saddened me to destroy his faith, but I told him the truth. I told him that I would have to have recourse to the only medicine that could help me—that of separating myself from the government. He tried to argue me out of it. He could not absorb the fact that the movement he had so much faith in had itself already been left behind by Fidel's personal revolution.

Painfully, during the next three days, I got out of bed whenever I was able and wrote my long letter of farewell to Fidel. On the thirteenth of October I decided to get up and take the letter to the United Nations post office to have it registered, and to bring a copy to *Bohemia Libre,* the Cuban magazine published in New York. The physical pain as I dragged myself from one place to the other was severe, but before that day was over I was beginning to be able to walk better.

My blood pressure continued low, however. I called the young doctor and told him that I had done what he had tried so earnestly to prevent, and that if he wished, I would free him from the obligation of treating me. He said no, he would be right over. Though he repeated this for several days he never came back, and I was without

248

medical assistance, living on Adrenalin pills, for the three days that the press, radio, and television descended on my apartment. It was the nightmare I spoke of at the beginning of this book. Yet this was as nothing compared with the bitterness I had to absorb as I learned through personal experience what fanaticism is, how it breaks every human bond and ethical feeling and tramples even memories, tramples everything.

On the same day that I mailed my letter to Fidel, he ordered the first executions of revolutionaries. My only compensation that painful day was the knowledge that I had finished my letter and sent it off still unaware of that horror, which was the final stone in a wall that he built and that must separate us forever.

My country, which Nature appeared to have fashioned for harmony, joyousness and peace, is full of grief. It is bloodstained and bankrupt. The firing squads and cries of "to the wall!" are sowing the sweet earth of Cuba with panic and tragedy. I am suffering with my unhappy island and have again identified myself with its long, patient agony. But my soul is at peace.